Brown Like Coffee

For Students

Who Think Outside the Box

.

Brown
Like
Coffee

For Students

Who Think Outside the Box

By

The List Guy

www.brownlikecoffee.com

Brown Like Coffee
Copyright © 2007

All scripture quotations, unless otherwise indicated, are taken from the Holy Bible, New American Standard.

Website: www.BrownLikeCoffee.com
E-Mail: jack@brownlikecoffee.com & jill@brownlikecoffee.com

Printed in the United States of America.

Dedicated to this generation of:

1. Facebookers (who love to connect with each other)

2. iPoders (who love to dance to their own music)

3. Starbuckers (who love to share a good cup of coffee with a friend)

4. Worldchangers (who love to think outside the box)

FAQ
(Top Ten Frequently Asked Questions)

1. Who is this book for?

It's for any student (or student aged person) or faculty who wants to be challenged to live for Christ in some radical ways.

2. What's up with the title?

Absolutely nothing. It's totally random. Some think it's a spoof, but not really. We're just trying to have some fun. Is that ok?

3. Why two covers?

Neither cover has anything at all to do with the title or purpose of the book. We just thought they were cool covers. So, it's obvious we're confused. But you benefit. Americans like choice. So, choose away!

4. Why not share your real name?

I don't think students like "self-promotion", do you? I have enough pride without putting my name on the book. Besides, what if you don't like the book? I don't feel I could handle the rejection! A little mystery never hurt anyone, right?

5. Why is everything in lists?

It's a real problem. I can't seem to write anything without putting it in a list. Maybe I'm addicted, I don't know. It's weird, because I'm a fairly disorganized person.

6. Do you have any real experience with college students?

Besides the six years it took me to get my college degree I have been involved in college ministry for almost 30 years. I have several college age kids of my own and have had students living with us for over 20 years.

7. **Are you really giving away all the profits?**

   Every bit of profit is going to mission efforts to take the gospel around the world. I promise I will not pocket one penny. So, thanks for buying this book. You are investing in the Great Commission. Spread the word!

8. **Are you an idiot?**

   Not totally. My understanding is that I was a moron when my college age sons were in high school. But it is amazing how my IQ has gone up since the guys entered college. Not sure what happened, but all of a sudden I went from uncool to cool in less than 24 months.

9. **Do you have any other thoughts?**

   No.

10. **Was this a list?**

    Yeah. I couldn't help it.

Brown Like Coffee
The List Guy

Note: This book is divided up into seven sections, each with a different theme and a type of coffee that seem just right for each other. So, go to a coffee shop, open up to your favorite section, order the coffee listed there, and enjoy!

Getting Started
Cup of Joe

Just plain ol' coffee. A cup of Joe is short for java and because every "common Joe" drinks coffee. Some say it dates back to the 1800's when U.S. Naval officers would drink wine while the rest of the crew were just offered...coffee.

So, we all begin at the same place in the Christian life.

Let's get started.

Three Lame Reasons to Go to College

IF YOU COULD SEE MY ACT SCORE, YOU WOULD NOT BE wasting your time reading this book. Let's put it this way: I did OK in school apart from anything that had to do with words or numbers. In fact, lunch and P.E. were my specialties. I too, along with a few geniuses, would turn my exam in after only 15 minutes (of the allotted 60). The crucial difference, of course, was that there was something actually written on their tests!

Yes, I went to college, but *why* did I go? Uhhhh…not sure, except to say that I didn't know *what* to do with my life after high school graduation, and besides, I wanted to show off my red convertible sports car to the beautiful sorority girls. Powerful stuff, huh? As you can tell, I did not allow my school work to get in the way of my education! How in the world did I make it through college?

Can you say, "Cliff Notes"?

Enough of *my* confessions; let's talk about you. You're under all kinds of pressure to go to college. Parents, teachers, friends—all of society is giving you verbal *and* non-verbal cues as to why the only option in life is to—GO TO COLLEGE! Even Google is putting the heat on.

I typed in "go to college" and 1,270,000 entries popped up. I then typed in "don't go to college" and only 40,336 entries appeared. That probably wouldn't qualify as hard core evidence, but aren't we often made to think that *everyone* goes to college? Well, think again. Out of the almost seven billion people in the world only about 1% are college students—a mere 70 million. About 16 million of them are in the good 'ol U.S. of A.

Let's hear from a real expert: Rocky L. is a 17 year old graduating senior at New Hampshire's Manchester West High School. In a recent school newspaper interview he stated, "Going to college is the most important decision of your life. College makes a huge difference in people's lives. Not going to college, to me, is a really stupid move." Well, Rocky, answer me this: Where in the Bible does it ever say to go to college? I have been a student of the Scriptures for over thirty years, and I have yet to find even a remote reference to this "most important" decision in all of life. God is completely silent about going to college. It's not a command from God, but simply a choice *we* make.

At this point, you might hear me saying that I'm against you going to college. Absolutely not! We will have three out of our five kids enrolled at the State U this year. But my desire for them *and* you is to think through *why* you are going to college. There are a few good reasons to go, but a host of lame ones. Here are three:

Lame Reason #1: Just to have something to do

In "Orange County", a Jack Black movie a few years ago, one of the characters explains to his persistent mother *why* he wants to go to college: "Because," he says, "that's what you do after high school." Some end up there simply because they think it beats mowing lawns, detailing cars, or asking, "Want fries with that burger?" the rest of their earthly existence.

Not sure what to do next with your life? Go to college! That's the knee jerk reaction for many 18 year olds. The fact is some people have a hard time charting their future. They need ongoing outside structure and find a lot of security moving from high school to college where the prof says to show up on MWF 9-10 a.m., read textbook pages 185-205, and write a five-page paper on Stalin's role in WWII. Fourth year UCLA political science major Antonio M. was asked the purpose of a college education: "The purpose of a college education is to give you a cushion before you hit the real world. It's like a pillow so you won't land on the concrete." Sarcastically speaking: what a man of destiny, power, and vision!

I know questioning the wisdom of going to college is politically incorrect, but you're exchanging four of the most prime years of your life! Actually, research shows its closer to 5.2 years to get your bachelor's; only 33% out of the whole University of Texas system finish theirs in four years or less. And remember, if you're part of the few and proud who *do* persevere to obtain a degree, you will spend at least 16 years in school—not counting kindergarten or graduate studies—before you even *begin* your lifetime profession.

Let me add this: If a young person doesn't really know why they want to go to college, I would probably counsel them to....go to college! Why? In hopes that they would rub shoulders with a few "purpose driven" followers of Jesus who know *exactly* why they're there.

Lame Reason #2: Just to meet the person of your dreams

Gentlemen, if you want to, I can just about guarantee you can find *someone* to marry you during your college years. But, in contrast to many Christian authors, I think 18-22 year old believers ought to be focused on *becoming* the right person more than *looking* for the right one. Most students, though, have lowered the bar still further. They're not even looking for the *right* person to marry; they're looking for *any* person to marry! My Bible says God put Adam to sleep and then took responsibility for bringing Eve *to him*. Think He's powerful enough to do it for you?

Ladies, are you at college to get your MRS. degree? April and May are not only beautiful female names, but also busy sales months at jewelry stores near universities. I've seen so many girls hit the senior year "panic button" as they jealously observe girls all around them getting engaged and there *they* are: little miss lonely with no one to put a ring on *their* finger. It makes a girl think and do some terribly irrational things—like chase and marry the next guy that comes along. It's not like you can wake up ten years later in bed, roll over and say, "Ummm, I need to tell you something.... I don't think I should have married you." It may not have *been* the will of God to get married, but when you tied the knot… it *became* the will of God!

I'm not saying you won't meet and marry the person God has for you in college. I can see, though, why stats show the longer a person waits to get married, the better the chance they'll *stay* married! I know. Both of my brothers got married in college. One lasted eight months, the other two years. Who you marry can make you or break you. I beg of you, spend your college years focusing on *becoming* the person God wants you to be more than desperately trying to find "THE ONE." Don't fret, trust God. He will bring along just the right person at just the right time. I know it sounds a little radical, but I propose you use your college years more for spiritual growth and ministry than for "mate acquisition."

Lame Reason #3: Just to make a lot of money

The *Princeton Review* humorously lists the three formulas every college student must know:

1. $e=mc^2$
2. nitro + glycerin + fire = boom
3. college = good job = tons of dough = happily ever after

Deep down people probably know making a lot of money won't make them happy—but they sure want to give it a try! If you're currently a student, have some fun with me as we take a road trip through the crevices of your soul:

"So, why *did* you come to college?" I ask in a laid back, casual manner.

"Well," you say proudly, "I'm here because I want to get a *good* education."

Sitting up in my chair, I respond, "Okay....but, *why* do you want to get a good education?"

"Mmmm," you ponder, "Well...because I want to get a *good* job."

Now I lean toward you and reply, "A good job, huh? Why is it that you want to get a *good* job?"

"Wait a minute," you shoot back, "I see where you're going with this! Okay, I admit it. I want a good job so I can get a better salary."

"Well, *why* would you want a better salary?" I slyly inquire.

By now you've probably decided the discussion is over with and I'm just hoping our friendship is not! Maybe the final destination of this interrogative joy ride revealed to you that you're going to college in order to get a good job, to make a better salary, so that you can....so that you can....what? Say it! *Support the kind of comfortable lifestyle you have always dreamed about!* This could be the exact motive your well-intentioned parents drummed into your brain, but can you see where it leads?

> **Life:** Should we follow the money or a divine mission?

> **College:** We know why our culture believes it's important, but what does God think?

Walt Henrichsen, the author of the classic book, *Disciples Are Made Not Born*, made this shocking statement:

> "If you are at college for any other reason than to be a
> missionary for Jesus Christ, you are there for selfish,
> sinful reasons."

Woahhhh! I'm glad he said it and not me! Did this former pastor and Navigator campus representative go *too* far in his challenge to students, or had he found an open nerve that desperately needed to be uncovered and dealt with? As I gaze down from my tree house, it appears a huge percentage of students, even "committed" Christians, are at college with a conscious (or sub-conscious) personal agenda that is selfish, yes, even sinful! Now that we've all had our greedy little hearts torn open and exposed, we must ask *the* definitive question:

Why are *you* at college?

For your purposes—or God's? To build up and advance your little kingdom—or His? To pad your resume—or to represent the person and purposes of Jesus Christ? I'm *not* saying you should neglect your studies, eliminate dating, or turn down a well-paying job. I *am* saying that we will stand before God someday and account for our time, our money…our life. Go to college, but don't get an "A" in school and an "F" in the Kingdom! Majoring in the eternal, rather than the temporal, will help insure a "well done My good and faithful servant" when we turn in our *final* exam.

The Box:
I've listed three lame reasons to go to college. Now you tell me. What are three *good* reasons to go?

Note: These end of the chapter little application exercises are TOTALLY optional. Kind of like adding cream and sugar to your coffee—it's up to you. Each chapter I include a personal question in "The Box" and then you are encouraged to think and create your own list—outside the box of course!

Eight Spark Plugs to
Get Your Motor Running!

IN THE MIDDLE OF A SWEAT-LADEN, BRICK-THROWING basketball game of Michael Jordan wannabes, some girl came running up to me and said, "LeRoy Eims wants to have dinner with you—right now!"

Well, LeRoy Eims was a hero of mine. He was a former marine officer, a successful staff leader for The Navigators campus ministry, and now author of one of my favorite books: *The Lost Art of Disciplemaking.* To get the chance to eat a meal with him and pepper him with questions was a dream come true. So, instead of launching one more air ball, I snatched up the four guys I'd been discipling that school year and sprinted over to the dining hall where "Mr. Eims" (as I respectfully addressed him) and all of us were eating our meals during this weekend collegiate conference.

I spotted his silver hair and chiseled face over in the corner eating at a table by himself. The five of us quickly grabbed our food and then, with great reverence, tiptoed over to Mr. Eims, asking permission to sit and drink of his wisdom. It was obvious, though, he was all business, so we dispensed with the introductions and small talk. I pulled out my neatly folded paper of carefully crafted questions to ask "the master"— but probably also with the motive of impressing my young disciples.

Tilting forward, attempting to initiate eye contact, I asked: "Mr. Eims…how can we be *sure* we are still walking with Christ twenty years from now?" Leaning back, so proud of my question, I anticipated him rattling off a string of verses or drawing out an intriguing diagram. Instead, there was nothing. He didn't even look up—just kept eating. Finally, I repeated the question, but before I could finish my sentence, he raised his fist, pounded the table and shouted, "Live for Christ *today*!" and then he immediately looked down again, quietly stabbing another batch of green beans with his mess hall fork.

Glancing left and right, I timidly dove back in. "Well, Mr. Eims," I nervously stuttered and stammered, "could you expand on that a bit?" Now afraid to repeat my question, we all just waited in awkward silence for him to digest his food—and my inquiry. Finally he looked up, pointed his finger at each of us and exclaimed, "If you live for Christ today, today will turn into tomorrow, and the days will turn into weeks, weeks into months, months into years, and years…into a lifetime!"

I'm sure we asked other questions that day, but my puny little brain couldn't absorb any more than one truth at a time. Good thing. Now, years later, I am *still* trying to apply this one blunt, but profound, piece of advice—one day at a time.

Live for Christ today!
Not tomorrow…TODAY!

It still rings in my ears.

Another year passing, another year beginning. They fly by much faster now, don't they? Why not make this year, this month, this week, this DAY different? Get off your duff and get going. Don't sit on that sofa one more minute, watching one more reality show, one more football game, one more DVD. Make something of your life. There are small steps you can take—right now! You can't steer a parked car, so let's fire it up, put it in gear, and get moving. Here's a short list of eight spark plugs that can help ignite your life—eight things you can do right NOW!

Spark Plug #1

Come to Christ if you haven't already. If not, I implore you to get down on your knees at once and turn your life over to Jesus Christ. It's not the position of your body, though, that matters—it's the position of your heart. Confess your sins to Jesus and make Him *your* Savior and *your* Lord. If you could know God in a personal way, would you want to? Of course! So don't wait one more minute to establish a personal relationship with your Creator. It will forever change your earthly *and* eternal destiny.

Spark Plug #2

Yearn for intimacy with God. Grab your Bible, go to a quiet, private place and get some TAWG (Time Alone With God). Set aside 15, 30, even 45 minutes and draw close to Him. Like Psalm 51, pray like King David did, "Search me, O God, and know my heart." Drink deeply from His Word, then pour out your heart to Him. There are some *good* addictions. This is one of them.

Spark Plug #3

Leave a destructive habit behind. Whether it's just unhealthy or downright sinful, let go of it before it won't let go of you. This is more than just a new year's resolution, this is a "do or die" decision you need to make. Freedom is not the power to do whatever you *want* to do, but the power to do what you *ought* to do. Ask the Holy Spirit to help you break the bondage of slavery to sin and then, today, make the necessary changes—so God can set you free!

Spark Plug #4

Initiate a conversation with a broken relationship from your past. Matthew 18 teaches that if there is someone who has something against you (or if you have something against them), stop—before you even pray to God—and go to them. It could be a family member, ex-boyfriend or girlfriend, maybe even someone back in your high school days. Visit, call, write, do *whatever* you have to do to say you are sorry for your anger and pettiness. Cleanse your soul by extending to them the same grace and mercy Jesus has to you.

Spark Plug #5

Nurture a younger believer. Look around you. Is there someone at your school, work, or church that needs to grow spiritually? Ask if the two of you can team up to grow together. If you're having a quiet time, you can help them start. If you're memorizing Scripture, show them how. If you're sharing your faith, bring them along. If you're plugged into a good local church, invite them to join you. You may not *feel* like you have anything to offer another believer—but you do. I believe the Biblical command to "be fruitful and multiply" is a spiritual as well as physical mandate. Go for it!

Spark Plug #6

Die to self. Don't let your world revolve around you. The happiest people I know are the ones who constantly serve and give to *others*. If you can't give away something, you don't own it. It owns you! Materialism is choking us, and most Americans don't even know the difference between our wants and our needs. Look around at all of your stuff. Give away something (maybe that you're really attached to) this week, just to prove to God (and you!) that *you* don't own it—God does.

Spark Plug #7

Eat a meal with an international student. Some say there are as many as 750,000 on U.S. soil, most of which will never even set foot inside an American home. They are the cream of the cream of the crop in *their* countries, but we ignore them, treating them as "nobodies." Want to impact the world for Christ? God has brought the future world leaders to our doorstep. Befriend just one student from another culture and begin to share your life and the love of Christ with them. It could change their life—and yours!

Spark Plug #8

Resolve to set goals; and this time…stick with them! After you finish your next meal, get the notepad out. Pray and ask God for wisdom. Don't just lazily say, "I want to be a better Christian this semester." Instead, SPAM yourself! Set challenging, but realistic goals that are Specific, Practical, Achievable, and Measurable. In Luke 2:52 Jesus grew physically, mentally, socially, and spiritually. Those aren't bad categories for us to set goals in as well. Then, ask a friend (who isn't afraid to throw tough questions at you) to check with you each week on how you're doing.

The first letter of each of these eight spark plugs spells C-Y-L-I-N-D-E-R. Eight good spark plugs will keep all eight cylinders in a car pumping away and moving ahead. I know… a little cheesy, but *anything* to help you remember my list!

As a college student, I once asked my father a dangerous question. "Dad, if there was one area of my life I need to work on, what would it be?" Without even a pause, he immediately shot back, "Oh, that's easy—procrastination." I tried to act shocked, but I knew he was right. He lovingly exposed my longtime, but immature, policy of: "Why do today what I could put off 'til tomorrow?"

My hair is not silver and my face is not chiseled, but if you and I could sit down and eat a meal together, I would probably just give you one piece of advice. You guessed it:

Live for Christ today!
Not just tomorrow…TODAY!

It still rings in my ears.

The Box:

Which of these eight spark plugs could you start putting into practice *this* week?

Ten Essentials for Every Christian College Student

ONLY 1% OF THE WORLD'S POPULATION IS COLLEGE students, and I commend you if you are one of the elite that represent us in institutions of higher learning. It is one thing, though, to start college and quite another to finish it. In fact, most drop out somewhere along the way, and just under 25% of Americans have actually completed a college degree. One reason students give up on college is because of "priority pressure", the constant stress of trying to choose what is good versus what is best. If you're currently a college student, I know your life is swirling around you like a Kansas tornado, but unless you want to be picked up and swept away like Dorothy and Toto* read and heed "The Ten Essentials for Every Christian College Student".

Essential #1: Choose a life purpose

It is a choice, and you get to make it. You have a free will, but an all powerful, all knowing, all loving God gave it to you. So, why not revolve your life purpose around the One that gave you life in the first place? Don't let one more *American Idol* show go by before you've nailed this down.

Lock your door, get your Bible out, and search. As a sophomore I came

*For those of you who grew up playing video games instead of watching movie classics, these are the main characters in "The Wizard of Oz."

up with: *"To glorify God through knowing Him and making Him known to others."* Not original, but it was mine. Having a God-centered life purpose gets you up in the morning, helps you make good decisions, and looks cool on your bathroom mirror!

Essential #2: Develop a biblical worldview

I'm reading an intriguing book by Chuck Colson called *How Now Shall We Live?* that's giving me a major paradigm shift. After taking two Tylenol, I admitted that I had a puny, self-centered worldview and forced myself to ask, "Am I looking at life from *my* perspective or from God's?" When we saturate our minds with the Word, we develop a God-shaped grid to run every song, movie, and idea through. Try Colson's daily worldview update at www.breakpoint.org.

Essential #3: Seek out the right friends

My pastor says, "If you're trying to follow Christ, don't choose as your best friend someone who is running from Him." Studies show at least 50% of students have cheated and don't think it's wrong, almost one fourth are frequent binge drinkers, and cohabitation (us old timers call it "shackin' up") is at an all time high. Be careful; getting tight with one of these folks could be more painful than watching a rugby game! I'm not saying don't befriend non-Christians, that's the key to drawing them to Christ. But bind your heart to someone who is *really* seeking God: "As iron sharpens iron, so one man sharpens another". Touche!

Essential #4: Join a good church

Away from home? No one to tell you to get up and go find one of those premium back row seats at the fam's church? *Now* you can prove what you're really made of! Micro scooter yourself over to the late service of that local fellowship that: 1) Teaches the Bible as the Word of God, 2) Has great worship, and 3) Welcomes you and your friends. Don't just sit and soak it in, though. Give some of your time, talent, and treasure to those folks. It will pay great dividends.

Essential #5: Form consistent study habits

I'm a total hypocrite even mentioning this one because I don't think I cracked a book until mid-way through my junior year! Yeah, you can buy tests and papers via the internet, and supposedly everybody does it, but why not keep your integrity intact? Besides, having a clear conscience *and* an educated mind is a powerful combination. As I "matured" in college, I started going to *every* class, sitting on the front row, and finding the top student to study with. Stay focused and you'll end up with more than just school loans to pay back—you'll have a college degree! Be all you can be!

Essential #6: Initiate personal ministry

To balance out #5, I must say: Don't let your class assignments dominate your life while in school. The biggest lesson you will learn at college is what God wants to do in your life and *through* your life. Find a group that's trying to witness and disciple others. Pray about living on campus, starting or joining a small group Bible study, sharing your faith and seeing God change some lives for eternity. If you really want to get radical, join the thousands of students who do short term summer mission trips. Look 'em up at www.ShortTermMissions.com.

Essential #7: Set up dating standards

57% of collegians claim they're "sexually active". Think this is just locker room braggadocios? Think again! Many are looking for sex without strings and relationships without rings. Millions of people are downloading their lovelife via online dating services. And here is a profundity: You *will* marry someone that you date! Commit yourself to only date others who have the kind of goals, faith and character you want in a mate someday. Think I'm being picky? Exactly!

Essential #8: Maintain a proper balance

Harry Potters' Professor Dumbledore sheds this light: "It is our choices that show what we truly are, far more than our abilities." Whether you like Harry's series or not, the prof's got a point. College is all about choices. With suicide now the third leading cause of death among college-age young people, it's time to adopt the four square life that Jesus sought in Luke 2:52: "He increased in wisdom and stature, in favor with God and man." Jesus chose not to sweat the small stuff, but instead to develop Himself mentally, physically, spiritually, and socially.

Essential #9: Appreciate your parents

Okay, so my wife put me up to this one. It is amazing, though, how much smarter your parents get once you leave for college! You begin remembering all their laborious lectures and suspect that maybe they did have a sliver of wisdom in those thick brains! And if you catch fire for Christ, don't make the mistake I did and go home and tell your parents they're going to hell. People most often become Christians through the witness of a family member. So call them. Visit them. Tell them you love and appreciate them; and if they oppose you getting branded with a "tribal art" tattoo hear them out!

Essential #10: Keep graduation in mind

Nearly one third of freshmen drop out of college their first year. Congrats if you are part of the remaining two thirds! Also, know that those with college degrees earn nearly twice as much as those without. But more important than a diploma or an extra zero on your paycheck is what kind of person you plan on being when you graduate. My definition of college?

A window of time God gives us to make critical decisions and prepare ourselves to live them out.

Set goals, seek the Lord, build a deep foundation and understand that how you finish your college career says so much more about you than how you started it.

Oh, and have some fun too!

The Box:
Which of these ten essentials are you strong in? Weak in?
Share 'em with a friend.

The Basics

Espresso

This is the key ingredient that all other coffee drinks are built on. Espresso is just coffee in concentrated form.

Jesus Christ is the key ingredient we build our lives upon. Nothing exotic, nothing mystical.

Just the basics of the Christian life.

Six Reasons Why I'm a Follower of Jesus

I DON'T LIKE THE WORD "CHRISTIAN". THE EVENING NEWS tells of Catholics and Christians killing each other in Ireland. History books teach of the 12th century "Crusades" where supposed Christians were killing Muslims, thinking they were somehow delivering divine justice and/or convincing them to convert to their style of religiosity. Some people, of course, will blame *any* and *all* atrocities on Christians, including the Spanish inquisition, persecution of Jews, Salem witch trials, even Tiger Woods' golf slump!

You have to admit, there is a lot of baggage with the word "Christian." It's one of the most misunderstood and over-used words in the English language. Here in the south, nine out of ten people you ask, "Are you a Christian?" almost instantly say yes. I did. I was 18, had a mother, went to church, had a bible, ate apple pie, believed in God and was even vice-president of my Fellowship of Christian Athletes chapter. But was I a real follower of Jesus Christ? No way. I did not know that a *personal* relationship with Jesus—the God of the Universe—was even possible.

Another case in point: Larry is a friend of mine who shares his faith with strangers. Out of curiosity (or insecurity) the person he is sharing with will almost always come back with: "What religion are you?" Larry, of course, knows what they're really asking, but he loves to string them along by telling them his religion is "bass fishing"—then he just waits for the confused look to spread across their face. At that moment Larry adds, "Oh, you may have been asking me about my relationship. My *religion* is bass fishing, but my *relationship* is with Jesus." He believes the Christian faith is not a religion at all, but a personal relationship with the living God; not some structured ceremonial hoops to jump through each Sunday morning, but a moment by moment dynamic intimacy with the Savior of our soul.

We need to help all people—even true believers—understand that being a Christian is not just a title or label—it is something you *are* and something you *do*—to follow Jesus. *Wherever* He leads. This implies lordship. A.W. Tozer, the famed pastor and author from Chicago, stated it well when he said,

"If Jesus is not Lord *of* all He is not Lord *at* all!"

So, maybe a re-definition is in order. Could it be that a real "Christian" is someone who is truly *following* Jesus?

Yes, I'm involved with my church, campus ministry, helping other groups through my writing and speaking, etc, etc…. but what am I *most* involved in? One word. Jesus. I am into Jesus. No other tag, title, or license comes close to competing. So, don't let the "extra stuff" that the American culture of spirituality promotes dominate you. God in the flesh never tried to impress anyone by playing their religious games—why should we? Give me the pure, unadulterated gospel of Jesus Christ. No more. No less.

This idea of "gospel plus" can get us in trouble. For instance: Where are we commanded to pray before meals? Or to dress up for church? Or to walk an aisle and join a church? Where does it say not to dance or drink wine? Adding "do's and don't's" to the gospel is a huge cross-cultural issue as missionaries attempt to bring Muslims, Buddhists,

Animists, and Hindus to faith in Christ. We are so regimented in our thinking that we insist Muslim converts use *our* word for God rather than theirs. We can't bear to see unclothed tribal people and so we make sure they have appropriate attire to attend the church buildings we have constructed. And, of course, you can't have church without a building, can you?

But Jesus meant to make the complicated simple. He wanted to cut through all the rules and regulations to get to the relationship, purposely putting all the goodies down on the bottom shelf where anyone (whether they be fisherman or Pharisee, freshman or Physics prof) could have the chance to understand and embrace Him. And His message? Two words:

Follow Me!

After the resurrection, on a lonely beach one morning, Jesus described to Peter the kind of martyrdom he was to endure. When He finished, Jesus fixed His eyes on the disciple and simply said, "Follow Me!" (John 21:19). But instead of saying "Yes, Lord" and accepting his destiny, Peter threw his own private pity party, wondering aloud why *he* would have to suffer such a cruel death, while the other disciple, John, would not. But there was to be no debate that day. The Master's final words recorded in John's gospel were to Peter when He once again (with emphasis) commanded: "You follow Me!" (John 21:22).

Some may say that feels like being drafted into God's army *against* your will, but in reality, it is an invitation to be a close friend and companion with the creator of the cosmos. Many so-called Christians strive to live religious lives out of the "ought to" rather than experiencing the freedom of following Christ out of the "want to." You'll want to go through this exercise of getting in touch with your own personal motivations, but besides the fact that God chose me (read Ephesians 1) here are at least six reasons why *I* choose to be a follower of Jesus.

Reason #1: I'm addicted to the love of God

I've never done drugs before, but mainlining big doses of the unconditional love of God is a life altering experience. To be able to truly say: "I like being with you—in your presence; it brings me pleasure" is just about the biggest compliment you can pay anyone. Being in a relationship with Jesus is a two way street. He enjoys you and He wants you to enjoy Him. Be still and drink deep from the delightful well of His endless love. I guess I'm hooked!

Reason #2: He has changed my life

I remember all too well what my life was like before Christ, and I don't want to go back to the emptiness I saw in my own soul and others. Helping people see their desperate need for Christ is no easy task. In my ministry, we work hard at helping students see they're lost before we can ever help them get saved. I believe the campus "hellion" is a lot closer to the kingdom than the good moral person who deep down thinks they are good enough to get into heaven. Me? I was a desperate man who took desperate measures. The payoff? Jesus Christ transformed my life—forever.

Reason #3: I don't want to go to hell

I want to go to heaven to be with Jesus, my family, and Christian friends forever. It's obvious from the gospels that Jesus believed in a literal heaven and hell. Ultimately God gives us what we choose. If we choose to live a life separate from Christ on earth, *that* is what He will give us for all eternity. But, by His grace and mercy God has extended the free gift of salvation to all true believers. What a comfort to be able to put my head on my pillow at night and know, beyond a shadow of a doubt, that if I were to die in my sleep, I would wake up in the presence of God.

Reason #4: I have a reason to get up every morning

As a high school senior, I remember waking up one morning thinking I must be the loneliest young man in all of America. Oh, I had the sports car, the girlfriend, the secret bachelor pad apartment with the tv/stereo, and all my "groupie-like" friends. I worshipped football so much I slept each night with one cradled in my arms. But all the time, money, and energies I was pouring into those pursuits did not give me the "kick" I was looking for. It wasn't until I humbled myself, said no to the world, and yes to Christ, that I found a real, lasting reason to wake up each morning. My life is not a bed of roses all the time, but at least I know what my mission is each day: to know Christ and to make Him known.

Reason #5: I don't have to be a slave to sin any longer

I had no way of conquering the sin in my life. I tried and tried, but to no avail. I turned over so many leaves in my life I looked like Sherwood Forest! I realized I can't change in my own power. A Christian hero of mine, Major Ian Thomas, used to pray, "Lord, *I* can't—but then You never said I could. Lord, *You* can—but then You always said You would." Give up. Surrender. Become a slave to Jesus and He will set you free. Oh, I still struggle with sin, but the Holy Spirit inside me is now my helper to break the chains.

Reason #6: Truth is very difficult to run from

I have studied the other religions of the world. None have a Jesus. None have a perfect God-man who died for our sins and rose from the dead. None have a salvation by grace through faith alone as the way to heaven. It is all by works. But how much is good enough? What about when you slip—do you lose your salvation? Other religions, cults, and works-oriented "Christian" groups have taken the truth and twisted it. I don't want to look back on my life and realized I based it on a lie. I ran from God and His truth long enough. Now, I'm running toward Him.

In the final analysis, the Christian life is not about me. It's about God and bringing glory to Him. It's not about God blessing me nearly as much as it is about me blessing God! His job is not to follow me around to fulfill my every wish. His desire is for me to set aside my own agenda for His. In fact, Jesus boils down our existence on this planet to two words:

Follow Me!

The Box:

Think deeply. List 2-3 reasons why *you* are following Jesus.

Seven Questions to Rock Your World

WHO IS THE MOST SPIRITUALLY POWERFUL PERSON YOU know? I'm not necessarily talking about someone who has a position of authority in a ministry, or even the person who has a ton of Bible knowledge. This individual has such a deep and authentic devotion to the person and purposes of Jesus Christ that everything they do, everything they say, exudes a profound spiritual authority. Like Jesus, they are *full* of grace and truth.

In contrast, the world is seeking a different kind of dominance, evidenced by a popular magazine that rates the top 100 most powerful celebrities on the planet based upon their wealth, how many magazine covers they're on, even the number of web searches for their name! It seems that a multitude of actors, athletes and business tycoons are stepping all over each other to get to the top of that heap.

How about you? What kind of power are you seeking? True power does not come from fame and fortune, but from God Himself. Psalm 62:11 says,

> *"Once God has spoken; twice I have heard this:*
> *That power belongs to God."*

If it's true that God is the only One that possesses real power, then we had better plug into *His* power source! The secret for obtaining this spiritual authority is as simple as "turning our eyes upon Jesus, and the things of this world will grow strangely dim", but to give you some handles to hang onto, I've crafted seven questions that I pray God will use to rock your world! Grab a friend, fasten your seat belts and prepare for impact!

Question #1: How do you view yourself?

One proud father was quoted as saying, "My son will do more than any other man in history to change the course of humanity. He's more charismatic, more educated, more prepared than anyone. He's the bridge between the East and West. There is no limit because he has the guidance. He is the chosen one. He'll have the power to impact nations, not people, but nations. The world is just getting a taste of his power."

The father? Earl Woods.

The son's name? Tiger.

As much as I am in awe of the way Tiger can hit the little white ball, I think dear 'ol dad went a tad overboard! My hope is that the son doesn't hold the same inflated opinion of himself his father does. Most of us don't have the problem of thinking too highly of ourselves, but rather too lowly. Struggling, wretched sinners is what many of us see in the mirror each morning. The key is not to view ourselves too highly or too lowly, but to see ourselves the way *God* does. Check out Ephesians 1:3-8 and discover that, as a child of God, you stand holy and blameless before your heavenly Father. So get up, dust yourself off, lift your hands to heaven and praise God that you are a "chosen one".

Bottom Line: Develop a Biblical Self Esteem

Question #2: What place does the cross have in your life?

Is it a Bible story you've heard so many times it's gotten old? Is it a hymn you've sung so often the words have become meaningless? Shake the cobwebs out of your brain for a moment and transport yourself back to the scene of the crime and stand (no, kneel) at the foot of the cross. In the midst of the crowd's cursing and crying, try to focus on the silent One in the middle, looking up into His eyes, full of pain, yes, but also love. Don't speak; just feel. Feel the cold, hard stakes driven through His wrists and feet and the blood flowing down. Feel the agony of being separated from His heavenly Father as He absorbs *your* sin into His very body.

Now, with your eyes riveted on His, pray this version of Galatians 2:20 back to Him, "Lord Jesus, I am being crucified with You, it is no longer I who live, but You who lives in me. The life I now live in the flesh, I live by faith in You, who loves me and gives Yourself for me." We need to understand that you and I deserved to be on the cross that day instead of Him. The only logical response to this ultimate act of mercy is for us to deny ourselves, take up our cross daily and follow Him. The cross: what place does it have in your life?

Bottom Line: Say No to Yourself, Say Yes to Him

Question #3: What do you count as significant?

Jack Welch, former President of General Electric Corporation and his wife, Jane, divorced several years ago. In splitting up the assets, they each submitted a budget that listed what they believed were the absolute bare essentials to sustain the lifestyle they've acquired. A sampling of Jane's *monthly* "needs" include: $7,500 for clothes, $2,500 for cell phones, $2,500 for dining out, $20,000 for travel, $1,000 for movies and opera, $10,360 for jewelry and $8,260 for wine.

I'm sure Jack's budget is just as ridiculous, but who is she kidding? We shouldn't scold her too much because most Americans, like Jane, don't know the difference between their wants and needs. In fact, you can perform an easy test on yourself to determine what *you* count as significant. Step one: Keep a detailed log this week on how you spend your time. Step two: Look at your checkbook and credit/debit card statements over the last three months. Step three: Prioritize these activities and items according to the most time and money spent down to the least. After finishing, you will be staring down at a piece of paper that reveals what *you* believe is important.

Bottom Line: Invest Yourself in the Eternal More than the Temporal

Question #4: Are you relying on your strength or God's?

When I travel overseas, the moment I step off the plane, I'm in charge. Why do I get to be the "instant leader?" Because I'm an *American*. Don't laugh, there's more. Not only am I an American, but I'm an *educated* American. On top of that, I'm a *sharp*, educated American! Do you think the locals there pick up on my blatant arrogance and egotism? It literally is dripping from me! Before you condemn me, though, take a look at your own heart. It is so hard for us to *truly* believe it when Jesus says in John 15:5b,

"Apart from Me...you can do nothing."

"Nothing at *all*, Lord?" That's right. Zero. The big goose egg. To be honest, sometimes I deceive myself into thinking that somehow, someway I'm clever enough to accomplish *something* in this world on my own apart from Christ. Moses forsook this kind of foolishness in Exodus 33:15 when he demonstrated the principle of relying on God's strength, not his own, praying, "If Your presence does not go with us, do not send us up from here." There's something greater than ourselves, even greater than our country. It's God. Rely on Him and Him alone.

Bottom Line: Lose the Arrogance and Abide in Christ

Question #5: What price will you pay for integrity?

The Josephson Institute of Ethics most recent survey claims that 74% of students cheated on an exam this year. 38% have stolen something from a store in the last 12 months, and 93% have lied to their parents. If these figures are correct, we are in the middle of a spiritual epidemic! It's easy to go with the flow, allowing the immoral stream of your campus to carry you along, but the tougher choice is to say, "Enough is enough!" and swim against the tide. You may lose a friend or two, but you'll like yourself better and certainly sleep more soundly at night! Acts 24:16 notes Paul's policy in such matters:

> "So I strive always to keep my conscience clear
> before God and man."

Whether it's test taking, tax returns or net surfing, who you are in private is…who you are! According to my pastor, one of the keys to keep a clean life is to allow the Scriptures to "wound" you on a daily basis, referring to Hebrews 4:12, "For the Word of God is living and active, sharper than any double-edged sword, it penetrates even to dividing soul and spirit, joints and marrow; and judges the thoughts and intentions of the heart." Verse 13 then gives the rationale for why we ought to simply surrender and allow the Word to pierce us to the core: "All things are open and laid bare to the eyes of Him with whom we have to do." God sees all and knows all and like a spiritual surgeon, He'll cut away *everything* that isn't Christlike in our life if we *truly* want Him to.

Bottom Line: Use the Word to Build Deep Convictions

Question #6: Do you really love others?

Anna had been happily dating Chad for almost six months before the bomb hit. She found out he had secretly started seeing Christy, one of her sorority sisters who had been e-mailing him notes and pictures of herself. It hurt Anna badly to see her relationship with Chad vanish as he and Christy became inseparable, spending every weekend together. In her quiet time one morning, Anna came across Ephesians 4:31 telling her to "Get rid of all bitterness, rage and anger…" followed by verse 32 exhorting her to "Be kind and compassionate to one another, forgiving each other, just as in Christ God forgave you." At that moment, she knew *exactly* what the Lord was telling her to do: release the anger and bitterness she held toward Chad and her friend Christy.

As the tears flowed, Anna felt the shackles fall off and the cleansing of Christ's forgiveness wash over her. With a new freedom and perspective, she set out to show kindness and compassion, especially to Christy, whom she was pretty sure was not a Christian. A few weeks later, a devastated Christy came to Anna's room after Chad had used her and moved on too. Christy was different though, now asking for forgiveness and seeking solutions for her shattered life. Late that night, because of the unconditional love she felt from Anna, Christy bowed her head and invited Christ to come into her heart as Savior and Lord. Now they became best friends, spiritually growing by leaps and bounds together. These two girls experienced the supernatural love and forgiveness of Jesus Christ in the face of a cruel and undeserved betrayal, and their lives would *never* be the same.

Bottom Line: The Love of Christ Changes Everything

Question #7: What will you leave behind in this life?

From 1989 to 1998 Prarie View A & M University obtained the not so distinct honor of being the worst college football team of all time. They may forever own this legacy, because during this ten year period, they lost eighty straight games! In 1991 they scored only 48 points the *whole season*, while their opponents racked up an average of 56 points *per game*! If you're a college student, you have the opportunity once you graduate to leave something behind that's more than just a win-loss record, a 4.0 GPA, or an impressive resume stashed in some school file.

Life is all about relationships and touching people for Christ. Some of the very last marching orders Jesus gave us were to "make disciples of all the nations" (Matthew 28:19). A woman came up to evangelist Billy Graham once, complaining to him about Dawson Trotman (founder of The Navigators college ministry) and spouting, "That Dawson Trotman, all he can talk about is making disciples, making disciples. He has a one track mind." Graham paused, looked at her wistfully and whispered, "Madam, I wish I could get on that same track!" Jesus Christ, along with Trotman and Graham's words, can motivate a new generation of students to take seriously this Great Commission and leave behind a legacy that will live on. Multiply *your* life by finding someone who can help you help others and then get started!

Bottom Line: Become a Disciple and Make Disciples

Epilogue: I recently had the privilege of traveling to the small Massachusetts town where the famous 19th century American evangelist D. L. Moody was born, as well as buried. Standing there by his grave, I realized that here was a man greatly used of God around the world and yet was uneducated and with speaking disabilities. Where did this former shoe salesman, who became one of the most spiritually powerful men on the planet, gain this depth of life and purpose? The secret might be revealed in a statement he would often make, "The world has yet to see what God can do through a man who is totally yielded to Him. I want to be that man." Moody sought the source of real power. Are you?

The *Bottom* Bottom Line: Power Comes from God

The Box:
Does your world need rocking? If so, which question(s) need to do the rocking?

Q #3, 4, 6, 7

Five Escape Routes
from the Matrix Maze

"THE MATRIX" WAS ONE OF THE COOLEST SCI-FI MOVIES OF all time. I just wish I understood it! Maybe the movie was a little like "Lord of the Rings" where you have to see it several times to *really* grasp the message. I felt sure the fog in my puny little brain would all be cleared up once I plopped down in front of Matrix 2 or 3, but no, the fog is still there!

I'm not usually one given to making disclaimers, but with a high degree of uncertainty I feel relatively sure that a possible premise in this movie *may* have been that everyone is trapped in a controlled, maze-like world with only a handful of people that know there is another reality that exists. But don't quote me on that. I could be wrong!

All the characters seem to be in a cosmic compound, going through the motions of a dream-like existence, doomed to forever be incarcerated by an artificial and mechanized life form (i.e. the bad guys) unless, of course, our hero, Keanu Reeves, releases them from their bondage, gives them an escape route, and shows them the "bigger picture." But, I remind you, if you could have seen my high school GPA, you would have serious doubts about my interpretation!

Whatever the meaning, I caught myself glued to the action thrillers, wanting to be a member of the tiny crew of "enlightened ones", rather than one of the millions of "blinded ones", and certainly not part of the computer generated, government type thugs like black suited Agent Smith.

Now, back to reality (I think), and in spite of our aspirations to super-hero status, most of us seem to be caught in our own version of the Matrix Maze. You might be feeling like you're confined in your own personal prison, with the freedom to do "what you *really* want to do" robbed by your parents, teachers, employer, maybe even God.

This huge, God-induced experiment called "Planet Earth" with billions of creatures labeled "Humans" might look like to you as the largest sci-fi flick of all time, where the Chess Master is moving us around like pawns on a board. But, the truth is reality is what God says it is and, as a result, we play by *His* rules.

You've heard it said that we don't break God's laws they break us! One non-negotiable is that He has given each and everyone of us 24 hours a day, 168 hours a week, and 365 days a year. Time is God's gift to us. How we use our time can be our gift to Him. Everybody *uses* time; some wisely, some unwisely. A *wise* use of this non-refundable commodity called time might be defined as:

Doing God's will for your life at any given moment.

Aren't you grateful that we have a loving, merciful, gracious God as our Creator and Lord and that He has given us not only a way out of our slavery to sin, but also the means to see things from *His* perspective? We can truly have the mind of Christ, get outside of the box, and think like He thinks. Here's the invitation to a higher plane that He extends to every believer: "If any of you lacks wisdom, he should ask God, who gives generously to all without finding fault, and it will be given to him" (James 1:5).

It's a simple plan: Ask God for wisdom, and He promises to give it to us. But most of us are just arrogant enough to think we can handle it on our own and bring about the necessary changes in our life that we desperately need.

Maybe you're like hordes of other people who, after getting fed up with the way they operated in the past, make a list of resolutions of how this upcoming semester will be different. Well-intended priorities and goals are set, only to be discarded weeks later as legalistic or unrealistic, ditching them to keep you from going....ballistic!

And if you're like most college students, your main complaint is that "I just don't have enough time!" There's *so much* you'd like to do, if only there were more hours in the day. Life is swirling around you so fast you can barely breathe. The age old adage always thrown at you, "Just wait 'til you get out of college, then you'll really be busy!" doesn't do anything but add to your depression.

Take a break in the action for a moment. Just for fun, get out your pen and take a little test with me (Don't worry, no prep required!) I call it a "Time Activities Analysis", and it will help you understand where all those precious hours are slipping away to. Take a typical school week and try to estimate how many hours you spend on each of these activities and write that amount in the blank (remember, total hours per *week*).

1. Social activities, dates, outings, etc... __10__
2. In-class time __18__
3. Homework __15__
4. TV and movies __2__
5. Reading (other than required for school) __1__
6. Physical exercise/recreation __5__
7. Sleep __40__
8. Preparing and eating meals __5__
9. Computer time (not school related) __3__
10. Personal hygiene (showering, make-up, etc...) __6__

11. Travel time   *5*

12. Personal errands   *3*

13. Work   *12*

14. Church/Devotional time   *4*

15. Personal ministry to others   *1*

16. Other stuff (anything else you can think of)

Total Number of Hours Listed   *130*

Now, let's do some math together. Add up the number of hours you listed on your "Time Activities Analysis" column and write it at the bottom. Below, take that same total and subtract it from the number of hours we have allotted to us each week (hint: 168). If it's a positive number, this represents the number of hours each week that are unaccounted for.

Total Number of Hours in a Week   *120*

Total Number of Hours Listed   *130*

Total Number of Hours Unaccounted for   *-10*

Even the most popular, time-crunched, responsibility-ladened students I've given this little quiz to seem to end up with 20-50 hours per week they *cannot* account for. It drives them crazy as they go back through their schedules and PDA's to scrounge up a few more hours here and there trying to prove to me just how busy, hectic, and stressful their lives really are.

Congratulations are in order, though, if you're the first student in history that can accurately report where all 168 hours of your week goes. But you'll have to keep reading with the rest of us mere mortals, because one small detail remains to be addressed:

Why did you use your hours the way you did?

I believe this will be the golden question asked of us when we come face to face with the Lord.

You may not have known that Moses wrote one of the Psalms, but in chapter 90, verses 10 and 12 he impresses upon us the necessity to use the time God has given us wisely:

> "As for the days of our life, they contain seventy years,
> or if due to strength, eighty years.
> Yet their pride is but labor and sorrow;
> for soon it is gone and we fly away." (verse 10)

> "So teach us to number our days,
> that we may present to You a heart of wisdom." (verse 12)

I had a roommate back in college who took this passage literally. He judged himself a pretty healthy guy, so he projected living eighty years and then, having applied the math and marking up his wall calendar, began working his way backwards, listing how many days he had left to live. There, staring at us each morning for breakfast, was a small box with a date in it and next to it a number such as: 21,361. The next morning we would find that number crossed out, only to be confronted with the next little date box on the calendar with the number 21,360 scribbled on it...and so on. Seeking obedience to Christ, he was numbering his days on his "World's Most Difficult Golf Courses" wall calendar, savoring each 24-hour period, in hopes that when He did meet His Savior in person, he would somehow be able to present to Him a "heart of wisdom."

Sometimes I feel like I have wasted so much of my time and in so doing, wasted so much of my life. Instead of getting under the pile about it though, I'm going to take the advice of pastor, teacher, and author Dr. Chuck Swindoll. His statement "It's *never* too late to start doing what is right" has always brought me a flicker of hope that I still have time to make my life count. In fact, Jeremiah taught us that the Lord gives us a fresh, clean, brand new slate each and every day: "For the Lord's loving kindnesses indeed never cease. For His compassions never fail. They are new every morning. Great is Your faithfulness." (Lamentations 3:22,23)

I just about fell out of my seat the very first time I heard that passage read out loud as a college freshman. I went back to my room to see if it was *really* there, to meditate on it, and to express gratitude to the Lord who gave me such an incredible promise. In the midst of all the painful, sorrowful lamentations Jeremiah was expressing, he could still see the awe-inspiring magnificence of a beautiful flower growing out of the dry, desolate ground. It could only be God's moment by moment, unfailing love in the midst of a dead and dying world.

In the next week or so, take a morning to get alone with God and His Word to determine what your priorities are going to be. Pray and think, and then set some challenging, but reachable goals that reflect the values that you *know* honors Jesus Christ. Make them as specific and measurable as you can, including a way (or person) to help you follow through with your commitments. Persevere through the year, not beating yourself if you miss a day or week. Get up, dust yourself off, and start again, knowing that either you (through Christ) will control your schedule or it will control you!

Well, we're at the end of the chapter and no lists. How can the List Guy not include an inventory of things to know or be or do? Look again. I *did* include them! Didn't you see them? They were buried within the text, almost like....a matrix! Don't tell me we're going to have to put mud in your eyes (like Jesus did in John 9) and ask you to go rinse it out so you can say, along with the once blind man, "I went and washed, and *then* I could see."

Close your eyes and look deeper. Let yourself go and *believe* they are there. Now step out in faith and recite to me what the five escape routes are to get you out of the Matrix Maze this upcoming year. That's it. Slow down your breathing, re-read the article, focus, and then make the list! I'll write it in invisible ink below so you can compare your answers (with the aid of your virtual goggles, of course).

Here they are:

1. **Ask God for wisdom and believe He will give it to you.**
2. **Know exactly where your time is going.**
3. **Count every day as a precious opportunity to think and live like Christ.**
4. **Start each morning with a fresh slate of the love of God.**
5. **Set and stick with your priorities, goals, schedule, and accountability.**

Oh, I forgot one!

This year just *enjoy* the movies.

Don't try to interpret them!

The Box:
Get honest for a second. Rank the top four priorities in your life. Why in that order?

1. ~~School~~ Family / Friends
2. School
3. Work
4 Faith

Thinking Differently

Cappuccino

Traditionally, one-third espresso, one-third steamed milk, and one-third frothed foam. For those developing a love for coffee this is usually the first drink ordered that is unique and special.

Stepping out in faith means trying something new— out of our comfort zone.

Let's start thinking a little differently.

Four "Must See" Fantasy TV Shows

Did I say fantasy? Sorry, I meant reality! I want to give two thumbs up for four awesome "must see" reality TV shows. You know the kind. A camera follows around a former bat-eating rock star and family to see what life is like in a "traditional" American home! Or, we get to tag along on twenty different dates of a beautiful bachelorette trying to pick between a host of panting suitors, only to find out later she ditched her newly crowned "soulmate" as soon as the cameras quit rolling on the season's finale.

Knowing that Americans watch an average of four hours of TV per day, let's take a huge leap of faith and assume our fellow citizens *can* tell the difference between reality and fantasy. For those who can't distinguish between the two, let's grab a Webster's for some help:

Reality—Not artificial, fraudulent, or illusory; genuine; a fact

Fantasy—Imaginative fiction featuring strange settings and grotesque character

You tell me. Are the shows being paraded in front of us each night reality or fantasy? Another definition I found of fantasy was "the process of creating unrealistic or improbable images." It's not only fantasy we are being fed, it's a whole dream world!

Enough sermonizing, let's find out what these four "must see" shows are! First things first, though. I need to make sure all of my living room furniture is appropriately arranged around the *real* American Idol, my wide screen TV. After setting myself in the big chair in the middle, I use my left hand to reach for the holy book of this pleasurable pursuit, my TV Guide. That, of course, frees up my right hand to cradle "my baby," the ultra-light, quick-touch remote control I bought with three easy payments after seeing it on a late night "you guessed it" TV infomercial. It's hard to be humble, but if remotes were like guns in the old wild west, I could outdraw anyone!

International death and disease is looming abroad, but at least we know that all is well here in TV land. The little screen (boy, is it getting bigger and bigger!) is bringing such joy and meaning into our drab and dull existence. And tonight will be the mother of all TV watchers' nights, as I just added the 24 hour "Reality Show Reruns" channel to my satellite dish network. I can't wait! It's a TV addict's dream. If *only* I had multiple screens where I could watch *all* the channels at once. I'm just thankful my remote allows me to instantaneously move from one program to the next. Okay, here's the lineup:

Fantasy Show #1:

Are You Hot? The Search for America's Sexiest People

It's a swimsuit competition where the only talent needed to win the $50,000 is the ability to turn around. The judges use a green laser pointer, called a "flaw finder", to point out (what they deem) imperfect body parts to the contestant....and to the twenty million *discerning* viewers. I'm sure that most of those twenty million are pre-med students, forcing themselves to watch in order to better understand human anatomy! Executive Director Mike Fliess, with such in-depth shows as The Bachelor and The Bachelorette to his credit, says that even he has to admit that "this is the most superficial show in TV history." Fliess says he tries to accomplish four things in his shows: sex appeal, fantasy fulfillment, an elimination process, and....humiliation. Mission accomplished, Mike!

Fantasy Show #2:
Survivor: Men vs. Women in the Amazon

Now the battle of the sexes goes to the Brazilian jungle to duke it out, for this classic edition of Survivor. The sixteen players are divided into the all female Jaburu tribe and the all male Tambaqui tribe. With all the estrogen and testosterone flying around, we'll be fortunate to survive this series ourselves! Survivor creator Mark Burnett thinks he knows the reason there's never been a love connection on their show: "Probably because they're completely smelly and, besides, who wants to make out with someone who hasn't brushed their teeth in a month?" Host Jeff Probst adds a pleasant thought as to why he thinks none of the contestants have ever found true love: "When you're not eating, you're throwing up!" If these descriptions of the show don't draw you in, then surely the anacondas, crocodiles, and piranhas will!

Fantasy Show #3:
Married by America

From the creators of *Joe Millionaire* comes another fascinating tale sure to stimulate meaningful conversation in the dining hall lines. Two single men and two single women, with the help of relationship experts, will have five potential mates selected for each of them. Family and friends will also get involved in the process, but ultimately the show trusts us, the viewing public, to vote on and decide which couples make the perfect match. One small detail: considering the astronomical divorce rate in this country, do these "marriages" have a snowball's chance in, uh....*Miami* to make it past the back doors of the TV studios? Why not give it a try, though? Just because they haven't found that special someone in their years of bar hopping and internet chat rooms doesn't mean they can't find them on national TV!

Fantasy Show #4:

World Wrestling Federation Smackdown!

Last but not least is the one reality show that has stood the test of time. This venue is not like the others. No, this is no "johnny come lately" fad that comes and goes within a month. Not only that, but tonight's installment is the WWF World Championship match (the third one this week!) where Hulk Hogan (the old guy on steroids) returns to answer the taunts of The Rock (the young guy on steroids). I've been watching this stuff since I was a kid, and I'm telling you they're bleedin' real blood and smashin' real chairs. This is no fantasy! You gotta' take my word for it. For this Smackdown rerun, I've even brought out all my WWF action figures one last time before I e-bay them all.

All four shows. All one night. This all so overwhelming, I'm getting a little emotional. Sex, greed, gambling, and violence. What more can you ask for?!

Okay, Okay, I know the Bible doesn't seem to condone some of these attitudes and actions, but can't we have just a *little* fun? TV is simply a reflection of our nation's values, right? You don't think it actually plays a part in shaping our thoughts or priorities, do you? Besides, I know it won't affect *me*. I've been a Christian my whole life and the two or three minutes I spend reading my Bible each day far outweigh any influence watching four or five hours of TV might have on me.

I can't understand why media commentator Robert Bianco of *USA Today's* Critic's Corner describes one of these shows like this: "It's a degrading, cut rate beauty contest that is about as vile a piece of televised sleaze as you're likely to find. It could have been merely harmless, if extraordinarily shallow, but fun turns into humiliation as the judges try to "out Simon" (American Idol's) Simon Cowell. Some will think it's funny. It's not. It's heartless, cruel, and in every sense indecent."

But just in case what he says has *any* truth to it, I have established a strong accountability safeguard for myself. To make sure that all these shows have absolutely no influence on me, I have cross stitched a verse of Scripture, framed it, and put it right above my TV cable box to review each night before all the prime time shows come on. Here it is:

> *"Don't let the world around you squeeze you into its own mold, but let God re-mold your minds from within so that you may prove in practice that the plan of God for you is good.."*
> Romans 12:2 (J.B. Phillips Translation)

I admit it. Deep down, I know that the Bible, not television, should be our constant companion, and the thing that "molds our minds." These "reality" TV programs are really just fantasy. Feeling a little guilty after a whole night of watching these shows, I blurted out in the presence of a friend, "What's the world coming to?!" He calmly turned to me without any expression and said, "An end."

"In the meantime" he added, "most people are grabbing onto *any* shred of fantasy or fulfillment this side of eternity. We don't want it to end. We want our little play world to go on and on."

It was only 1 a.m. (and the night was still young), but my friend flipped off the TV, looked at me and said, "Truth is, we are just passing through. This life is a testing ground. Heaven *is* reality, forever living in the presence of the One who made us. He *alone* defines and consummates all of reality. He laughs, and cries, at our pitiful little attempts to find meaning outside of Him."

His words really impacted me. I may have even shed a tear. But before I could get too convicted, my left hand (with my TV Guide in it) started to twitch uncontrollably. It then began sending urgent messages to my right hand (clutching my quick draw remote) commanding it to do a little channel surfing. Unbelievable, but true, and just in the nick of time, I was able to "peruse and choose" from these mouth-watering rerun options:

- *"The Pulse: Real Life Internet Dating Stories"*
- *"I'm a Celebrity—Get Me Out of Here!"*
- *"Scare Tactics"*
- *"The Bachelor 5"*
- *"Extreme Makeover"*
- and my personal favorite: *"Elim-a-date"*

Man, I'm like a kid in a candy store! Is this a great country, or what?

The Box:
Make a list of a few TV programs you have absolutely *no* business watching.

- The bachelorett/Bachelor
- You

---

*A note of full disclosure. I know it sounds totally weird, but the List Guy does not even own a TV. It sucked his brain out as a kid and he has never recovered.

Three Mysterious Words
To Move You from Death to Life

I WAS SITTING AT THE BACK OF THE CLASS SO AS NOT TO take up a seat of the truly "scholarly" students. These were the eager beavers who were looking for their next academic challenge, and had found it in this prestigious, and oh-so challenging seminary.

I don't remember the topic that particular day, but it must have been another deep and mystical doctrine, a complex and eternal theological concept, sure to spur the imagination of any true "John Piper wannabe."*

As the professor was scraping the Milky Way with his lofty rhetoric, one bookish, but clean cut young student with a three piece suit on, raised his hand and inquired,

> *"Fascinating thoughts professor, but how did Calvin's belief in limited atonement affect the other reformer's doctrine of supralapsarianism?"*

Everyone acted like they knew exactly what the student was asking, nodding their head with approval at the profound question just asked by their fellow deep thinker.

---

*Dr. John Piper is a great preacher, author, and thinker and speaks at all the PASSION collegiate conferences.

I wasn't dressed near as impressive with my "hand me down" blazer, corduroy pants and chukka boots. Nevertheless, I too was entitled to ask a question, wasn't I? So, after listening intently, taking copious notes, and scratching my head a bit, I asked, "Prof, tell me, how would you go about explaining this to a new Christian you were trying to help get established in his faith?"

You could have heard a pin drop.

The only sound that followed was the simultaneous turning of every head in the class, looking back to see what kind of simpleton would ask such a petty and inappropriate question. I was a little nervous, now being the center of attention, but I was able to keep my eyes focused on the instructor, trying hard to convince everyone that my inquiry deserved an answer.

So went my seminary career. As you might guess, I was the proverbial fish out of water.

My Senior Theology class professor got it right, though. He passed out a single sheet with 20+ theological terms (long and multi-syllabic words designed to intimidate any layman) and gave students one hour to write out a definition and explanation of each term as if we were explaining it to a *five* year old. Now, if you can explain "propitiation" so that a five year old can truly understand it…so do you!

There were three words on that list that stood out to me as absolutely critical. These three aspects of our salvation are mysterious, yet powerful, words that move us from hell to heaven and from death to life. I know you are much more theologically advanced than the average five year old, but for old time's sake, indulge me as I attempt to dramatize these three key Biblical concepts as simply as possible:

Mysterious word #1

Eric grew up in church, robotically attending all the worship services and youth meetings his parents had required him to. But, when he graduated from high school, he loaded up his car and headed out west, as far from his parents' religion and rules as he could get. He immersed himself in the party life of the university he enrolled in, totally rebelling against the wills of his parents—and God's.

"Why do you *always* have to talk about Jesus and the Bible?" he shouted out to his college room mate, whom he was sure was strategically placed there by his over controlling parents. "I don't try to push my beliefs on you, why are you cramming yours down *my* throat?" he added to his now quieted, but unwavering room mate who, by the way, was "randomly" assigned to him.

What Eric didn't realize is that God so completely loved him that He would continue to bring a witness into Eric's life until the young man turned from his sin, and placed his faith in Jesus Christ as his personal Lord and Savior.

Early one morning, as Eric's girlfriend was slipping out the back door, and he was coming out of a hangover from the previous night's beerfest, he happened to turn on the TV. Somehow the religious channel popped up and staring back at him was the same verse of Scripture that hung on his mother's mirror back home:

**"He made Him who knew no sin to be sin on our behalf,
so that we might become the righteousness of God, in Him."
(2 Corinthians 5:21)**

Eric thought he was in a dream because he began picturing himself on the ground, being tied to a cross, and crying out in pain: "Why am I here? Why am I here?"

Through his tears he peered up from the cross, where a man stood there, compassionately looking right into Eric's eyes and softly saying, "Because you deserve to be here. You have sinned against God and the penalty is death."

As the executioner raised his hammer to pierce Eric's body with his huge nails, the man once again spoke, this time stopping the soldier and whispering, "Take me instead."

The burly Roman soldier laughed and said, "Fine with me…fool!" He then turned to Eric, untied him and spouted, "Looks like your lucky day, kid. Run for it!"

At that moment Eric came to his senses, in a total panic and with sweat pouring off his brow. He then fell to his knees by his bed, realizing the man in his dream was Jesus Christ, the perfect and holy Son of God. He couldn't run anymore….Eric was the one who deserved to be on that cross, but the innocent and blameless God-man inserted Himself as the substitute.

The greatest exchange in all of history took place that day. The sinless Jesus actually *became* sin—for Eric. That day, sinful Eric became righteous—in Christ. Instantaneously, when Eric put his faith and trust in Christ he was made holy in the sight of God.

Now, Eric will forever be a child of God, saved from the penalty of sin.

It's a mysterious word called *justification*.

Mysterious word #2

Amber, a track star at her college, became a Christian one night in her dorm room; no angels, no trumpets, not even any goose bumps. She was simply reading from her New Testament where Jesus said, "Truly, truly, I say to you, he who hears My word, and believes Him who sent Me, *has* eternal life, and does not come into judgment, but has passed out of death and into life." (John 5:24)

She did believe. And, as a result, she accepted Jesus' promise that she had *already* passed out of death….and into life.

It was a done deal.

God had immediately bestowed salvation to her, and she was certainly looking forward to the heavenly home Jesus promised. But, she thought, what happens between now and then? What is she supposed to do with her life? How is she to develop this new relationship with God?

She decided the place to start was prayer. "Lord" she began, "I can't grow in my own strength. I need Yours. I ask You to fill me with the Holy Spirit so that I can live a life that is honoring to You."

Amber had heard testimonies from others how, once they became a Christian, life was an easy, painless bed of roses. But not so for Amber. In fact, it was a daily struggle. Some mornings she woke and felt like God wasn't even in her life. She constantly battled some of the old sins that beset her prior to her conversion. The more she read the Word, the more she understood that she had an enemy, Satan, who didn't just want to distract her, but *destroy* her.

She knew that God wanted her to be more and more like Christ each day, but it seemed like it was always three steps forward and two steps back. At the end of her rope, Amber had no choice but to totally throw herself at God's feet: "You and You alone can give me victory, Lord. I can see this is going to be a lifelong challenge of trusting You and Your power to conquer the trials and temptations that confront me at every turn."

She bowed her head and repeated out loud,

> **"But thanks be to God, who gives us the victory**
> **through our Lord Jesus Christ."**
> **(1 Corinthians 15:57)**

Finally standing up, Amber lifted her face toward heaven, understanding for the first time that the Christian life was a marathon, not a sprint. She was in it for the long haul, forever determined to keep growing in faith, hope, and love.

She was trusting God to give her victory over the power of sin.

It's a mysterious word called *sanctification*.

Mysterious word #3

When Sean died and stood before God, the Lord asked him a very hard question: "Sean, why should I let you into My heaven?" Frantically, Sean began racing through his past, thinking of all the times he had gone to church, put money in the offering plate, read his Bible, and even gone on mission trips.

He then recalled one of his memory verses which stated, "For by grace you have been saved through faith; and that not of yourselves, it is the gift of God; not as a result of works, so that no one may boast." (Ephesians 2:8,9)

Realizing there was absolutely *nothing* he could do to save himself, he quickly abandoned his listing of good works and blurted out to the Lord, "You *shouldn't* let me in!"

"What?" God asked.

"That's right, Lord", Sean replied, "You shouldn't let me in. I *want* to come in, but I have sinned and am I imperfect and I know would just mess up your sinless and perfect heaven."

At that moment, Sean called to mind one more verse,

"In Him, we have redemption through His blood, the forgiveness of our trespasses, according to the riches of His grace which He lavished on us." (Ephesians 1:7)

Instantly, Sean spoke up, "But…Lord."

"Yes, my son." God responded.

Pointing over to the Lord Jesus Christ seated on His throne, Sean called out, "Father, *your* only Son, Jesus, promised that if I would believe in Him and His death on the cross, that His blood would pay for and cover *all* of my sins. I get to come in to be with You forever, not because of *my* good works, but only because of the perfect blood of Christ *completely* covering me."*

The Father stood up with understandable pride. He waved Sean over and gave him a hug. "Come in my child. I don't see *any* sin or imperfection in you. You are holy and blameless in My sight. All I see is the gracious, merciful blood of Jesus that has washed you clean. Now, let Me just give you a taste of the delights of living with Me for all eternity."

For sure, Sean will forever be with the Lord, saved from the very *presence* of sin.

It's a mysterious word called *glorification.*

Three mysterious words to get you from death to life:

Justification—saved from the *penalty* of sin.

Sanctification—saved from the *power* of sin.

Glorification—saved from the *presence* of sin.

The mystery, though, is all wrapped up in the gospel. Have you experienced it?

> "To whom God willed to make known what is the riches of the glory of this *mystery* among the Gentiles, which is Christ in you, the hope of glory." (Colossians 1:27)

The mystery. Is it in you?

The Box:
Give three reasons why you are 100% sure that Jesus Christ lives in you.

*totally, absolutely, forever

[handwritten:]
- How I feel when I worship
- The fulfilment I get from church/Bible study
- I recognise my sin + see others

Three Professors from Hell

MAYBE YOU'VE CRUISED PAST THAT CHURCH MARQUEE IN the middle of a sweltering summer afternoon that read:

YOU THINK IT'S HOT *HERE*?

For some reason, making light of such a heavy topic just doesn't seem right.

Hell. It's not a popular subject these days. No one wants to talk about it, much less go there. I have a friend who actually wrote a full blown, hard back book on hell. Needless to say, it wasn't a bestseller!

Part of me wants to forget I ever heard the word. I don't want to believe there is a place of eternal torment that non-believers will spend suffering— forever. Besides, I want people to like me. I don't want them to view me as a weird fanatic that spews forth intolerant doctrines left over from the dark ages. I want to be cool, hip, with it—especially to the next generation.

But the other part of me desperately wants to share the gospel with everyone I can in order to save them from the terrible consequences that accompany their rejection of God's love.

Heaven and hell hang in the balance in many university classrooms across the world. Thousands of professors are modern-day Pharisees, not desirous of discovering the truth, or even teaching objectively. Instead, they push *their* agenda, searching for converts to their humanistic way of thinking. Jesus didn't respond too kindly to these type folks:

> *"Woe to you, scribes and Pharisees, hypocrites! For you travel land and sea to win one proselyte, and when he is won, you make him twice as much a son of hell as yourselves."* Matthew 23:15 (NKJV)

Jesus might very well label these so called educators, "professors from hell." Some slyly seduce students to open up their minds to all forms of "truth." Others love to chew up young, innocent Christians and spit them out—just for sport! The college classroom *is* a modern day battlefield for the hearts and minds of millions of impressionable coeds. Check out these three case studies from "down under!"

Professor #1: The Bully

With his long white goatee and hand carved cane, this prof liked to make a slow, deliberate entrance into his classroom. In the first few days of each semester he would defiantly challenge the Christians in his class to stand up—and thus *prove* their allegiance to Jesus. He then proceeded to rip them to shreds, seeking to destroy every cherished belief these young believers held dear.

One by one, they sat down, feeling embarrassed and defenseless in the wake of these scorching assaults by the esteemed doctor who had more degrees behind his name than they could count. His thick glasses, brown cardigan sweater, and long pointy fingers only added to the authoritative mystique he tried to create.

After 45 minutes of non-stop, blistering attacks, a young freshman girl was the only one left standing, determined not to sit down in spite of his now face-to-face hostile condemnations. Totally exasperated, the professor finally blurted out, "I have read the *entire* Bible. It doesn't make a bit of sense. How in the *world* can you believe in such a confusing, outdated document?"

All eyes were turned toward this petite, but now highly respected Christian student; everyone straining to hear her response to the professor's question. "Well sir," she began, looking directly at the man, "I can tell you *why* you didn't understand it. You see, the Bible is a love letter from God—to *His* children. I guess that's what you get for reading *other* people's mail!"

Stunned, the large class erupted into laughter and applause. Even the professor, with all his pontificating, realized the little girl with the big heart had bested him. He gave her a nod of admiration, turned to the class and said, "See you on Monday"—and walked out.

Professor #2: The Charmer

Handsome and preppy, this young religion prof was a hit with almost all his students. Not only did he write volumes on caring for the environment and animals, he'd recruit everyone he could to join him in his "feel good" causes. "God is everywhere, in everything, in every moment," he would say with such compassion and conviction. "He loves you, He loves the animals, He loves that tree," gently pointing toward an evergreen outside his book-laden office.

His greatest moment of triumph each year was his "any boat will get you there" sermon to the students. His theory was that all humans live on one side of a giant river and the afterlife is on the other side. "We will *all* get to our 'heaven' or 'nirvana' or whatever you want to call it—no exceptions. The only question will be *how* we get across," he confidently assured his listeners.

His crowd pleasing solution was that most will hop on the big ships (like Christianity, Judaism, Islam, etc...), others will choose the medium size boats (Native American religion, Wicca, etc...), while a few creative souls will simply design their own little "self-made religion" rafts and paddle themselves across.

On one occasion my Pastor was asked by some students there to present the "Jesus is the only way" perspective. And so, he publicly challenged this prof by saying, "If you're right and I'm wrong, then *all* of us are in good shape, regardless of what we believe. But, if I'm right, and you're wrong—then you're in a heap of trouble!" and then he quoted Jesus in John 14:6:

"I am the way, the truth, and the life.
No one comes to the Father, but through Me."

Not wanting to lose his influence with the students, this handsome, captivating prof quickly countered that *anyone* who hadn't been living under a rock the last 100 years would surely agree with him that there are *no* absolutes. Sitting at the back, I slyly lifted my hand and asked, "Are you *absolutely* sure about that?"

Naughty me!

I couldn't resist!

Professor #3: The Revisionist

This middle-aged professor (and school chaplain) with his dark, bushy, walrus-like mustache and rounded glasses, considered himself quite the academic. His most recent accomplishment had been completing a commentary on the book of 3rd Timothy (man, did I feel ignorant—I thought there were only *two* letters to Timothy!). He scoffed at my antiquated form of Christianity where I simply read the Bible and accepted it as God's word.

He, instead, chose to follow "higher criticism", subscribing to the conclusions of a world renowned group called *The Jesus Seminar*. This self-appointed collection of 30 supposed "scholars" sit around a large table and evaluate different statements in the gospels traditionally attributed to Jesus. After reading and debating a passage as to its validity, each person gets to cast their vote. They choose between four different colored pebbles in front of them:

Red: Jesus *undoubtedly* said this or something very close to it.
Pink: Jesus *probably* said something like this.

Gray: Jesus did *not* say this, but the ideas contained in it are *close* to his own.

Black: Jesus did *not* say this.

The group then tallies up the votes and—wham, bam, 'scuse me ma'am—you *now* have a sure-fire system to help you distinguish between what belongs in the gospels...and what doesn't! These self-described "fellows" (sounds a little sexist to me!) have gone the extra mile for the unenlightened masses by creating for us their own "Red Letter" version of Matthew, Mark, Luke and John—including only those verses that *truly* belong there. The problem with this game is that the majority rules, and the red pebbles won out on only 6% of the passages in our beloved gospels. Who knows, maybe it's all a marketing ploy in order to create and sell the "ultra thin" Bible that fits on your thumbnail!

These "humble" servants have concluded that the Bible is inspired in spots—and they're inspired to pick out the spots! This, dear friends, is the epitome of arrogance. In response, I shall not stoop so low as to make a reference to their founder's name (Robert Funk) and somehow imply that it describes the willy-nilly fog these people operate in. But I do wonder how these self-proclaimed intellectuals would vote on Revelation 22:19—not by coincidence, part of the final verses in the New Testament:

> *"If anyone takes words away from this book of prophecy, God will take away from him his share in the tree of life and in the holy city, which are described in this book."*

I'm afraid their high falootin' search for the "historical Jesus" will last a long time. In fact, it will last clear into eternity when, on judgment day, they will finally meet the Jesus of history...face-to-face. Philippians 2:10-11 teaches:

> *"That at the name of Jesus every knee should bow, in heaven and on earth and under the earth and every tongue confess that Jesus Christ is Lord, to the glory of God the Father."*

By that time, though, all the voting will be over with, and I think our *Jesus Seminar* friends will be shocked their revered colored pebbles didn't matter one whit. What counted was simply a "yes" or "no" to the King of Kings and Lord of Lords. Jesus will not waste any time by asking, "Who do scholars say that I am?" Instead, He'll be too busy giving us His own version of the *Jesus Seminar*, revealing His glory, radiance, power—and judgment.

Epilogue:

Sad to say that sometimes, we Christians are no different than the *Jesus Seminar* bunch. We look at Christ as if we're ordering a new SUV. "Let's see…give me the sunroof, CD player, and bucket seats, but leave out the chrome wheels and window tint." We pick and choose what parts of Jesus we like, thus attempting to create *our own* version of the Son of God.

Sorry, it's an all or nothing proposition. Either we believe and receive the Jesus of the Bible—or we do not. It's really very simple: He is both Savior *and* Lord and we do not get to divide Him up into little pieces, embracing some—and tossing out others. You better cast your vote now. I don't want you to be surprised like these professors from hell who:

"Professing to be wise, they became fools."
(Romans 1:22)

The Box:
Think of three profs you would like to share your faith with either publicly or privately.

Prof. Buffington
Alison Schofield
Dr. Hurt

Three Professors from Heaven

PROFESSORS. CAN'T LIVE WITH 'EM. CAN'T LIVE WITHOUT 'EM! Some drive you up the wall and others are sheer delight. Most of the classes (and the professors) you have will quickly fade from your memory in the next several years. But, there may be one or two teachers who make such an impact on you that you will never, ever forget them. In fact, you might just learn something from them that you'll take with you the rest of your life. Described below are three instructors that, at first, appeared to be professors from hell, but in the end, became for me like angels from heaven. I will always view them truly…as a godsend.

Professor #1: The Witness

The first day of class, this state university speech communications instructor looked young enough to be a student, and reinforced the impression by asking us to call him "Dan." His small stature, high-pitched voice and geeky appearance made me think this *supposed* professor was a real loser. Little did I know that in the next 20 minutes my initial disrespect for him would turn into profound admiration.

Skipping the obligatory perusal through the class syllabus, he dove right in with some examples of "speech communication."

"What are the different meanings of the word 'run'?" he asked.

After several responses, he then casually offered another example, "Well, how about some different meanings for the word…. 'christian'?"

After some rather weak, even embarrassed answers, he chimed in with *his* definition. He then followed it up with his personal testimony of how he came to Christ and the transformation that took place in his life. As he described in detail his personal relationship with Jesus Christ, I sat dumbfounded. Being a new Christian and a freshman, I didn't think you could get away with what Dan just did at a state campus. He shared his faith, though, with such ease and warmth, that almost no one noticed—or protested.

I immediately went up to him after class and told him I was a Christian too. He then, with a sparkle in his eye, asked, "Well then, why didn't you say anything in class today?" I didn't have an answer for Dan, but I was determined to be bolder for Christ from that day on.

Later that week Dan told us the word "encourage" meant to "put courage into." I then realized his willingness to openly share his faith had poured huge amounts of courage into *my* soul and I had a chance to prove it the very next Monday. It was the day the traveling campus evangelist, "Brother Jed", was making his annual appearance at our university. Standing atop the big fountain in front of the student center, and spouting his version of the gospel, he was ticking off almost every one of the 200 jeering and mocking students gathered around him.

I did not agree with all his doctrine or attitude, but I was extremely impressed by his boldness. Sitting there right in front of him, I watched and listened for hours on end, not even remembering I had classes that day. At one juncture in his fevered preaching and pointing, he stopped and inquired, "Does *anybody* want to give a witness today?" Instantly, and without asking my brain, my right arm shot up. Brother Jed invited me up on the fountain where I proceeded to share my personal testimony. As I surveyed the listening crowd, who did I see but Professor Dan, who'd just come from the class I had skipped!

Instead of angry looks for missing his lecture, he gave me smiles and nods of admiration. At that instant, as I was nearing the end of my sermonette, I sensed Dan was very proud of me. He should have been. His example of unashamedly identifying with Jesus Christ had been the spark I needed to ignite my faith—and my witness. Surely, he was…a godsend.

Professor #2: The Lover

I sat at the back of the state government class because my interest level was low, but even more so, because my friends were back there. A lovely, but very proper, older black woman named Mrs. Richardson was our professor, and instead of calling me by my (preferred) middle name, she insisted upon calling me by my first name, Leslie. In spite of my constant protests (and the girls at the class chuckling at me), she would respond to my raised hand by saying, "Yes, Leslie. What would you like to say?"

Finally fed up one day, I blurted out, "Mrs. Richardson, if you keep calling me by my first name, I'm going to start calling you 'Ruby'—your first name." It was an appropriate name, given the bright red lip stick she wore each day to compliment her perfect teeth and crystal clear word enunciations. So, each time she called me "Leslie", I countered with a "Yes, Ruby!" Instead of being terms of antagonism, though, it became a way to express affection for one another. I could tell she liked me, even though we were about to embark upon a semester long verbal battle.

One of Ruby's teaching methods was to allow students to do extra credit papers on a variety of topics related to government. I kept volunteering to do one until she finally relented and assigned me to prepare and present a paper (with a topic of my choice) the following

Wednesday. As I stood to read my essay, I knew my lovefest with Ruby was about to be tested. Her eyes (as well as the other students) grew wide as I announced the title: "The Ku Klux Klan."

Honestly, I do not know what possessed me to choose and research that topic. Incredibly, Ruby sat on the front row, listening with rapt attention, expressing interest and taking notes. When I finally sat down, she said, "Thank you, Leslie" and went on with class. Now getting a chance to reflect on my topic and paper, I was sure Ruby would give me an "F." But when I got my paper back the next day there was not only an "A+" at the top, but a second "A+" right next to it. She had actually *doubled* my extra credit because of my paper and presentation!

I sat at my desk stunned. I checked my grades once again and then looked up at Ruby standing by her desk. Her sly smile and twinkle in her eye let me know she loved me in spite of my foolish immaturity. Her character was shining through as she absorbed any pain I might have dished out during my speech, and instead offered me grace in exchange.

That day an older black female professor and a young white male student bonded. She modeled to me unconditional love in the face of humiliation. I certainly deserved retaliation and retribution, but got warmth and kindness in its place. I learned a lot more than state government that semester. I learned that age and race and gender and titles do not need to separate people. I learned that love covers a multitude of sins—my sins. Finally, I learned to call Ruby, "Mrs. Richardson". Now it was my way of telling her how much I loved and respected her. You see, for me, she will forever be…a godsend.

Professor #3: The Warrior

He paced back and forth like a soon-to-be father caged up in the hospital delivery waiting room. This administrative management professor with the bald head, big chest, and intimidating scowl would rant and rave, trying to motivate us students to think more deeply.

Like a buck private at boot camp, I dared not sit any place but front and center to glean all the keen insights Dr. Johansen gained from his thirty years of running corporations.

Constantly reeling off case studies to simulate business problems to be solved, he liked to put a student in the "hot seat" by whirling around, pointing his finger at someone, and demanding they give him the solution to the company's dilemma he'd just described. As a result, everyone sat terrified and petrified, fearful that Dr. Johansen would call on them to respond. With his Ph.D., CEO demeanor, and drill sergeant teaching style, I felt sure this was one of the most hardened, arrogant profs I had ever met up with.

One day he was role playing as the new owner of a huge livestock company in Wyoming who'd just purchased the company, thinking it was financially sound, when in fact, it was in deep trouble. He'd been told there were giant herds of healthy cattle in various parts of the state, but it was a scheme to get him to buy the struggling firm. Spinning around, and aiming his long finger at me, he said, "*I* am the sole owner of this cut rate cattle company, and *you* are my management consultant. What do you tell me now?"

I paused, looked down, looked to the side, and finally up into his death stare. I then calmly said, "Dr. Johansen, it appears to me that *somebody* gave you…a bum steer!" The class erupted in howling laughter, and even the professor, in all his glory, finally cracked a small smile. For a moment there, I thought I caught a glimpse of a sense of humor, maybe some personal warmth, possibly even a slight degree of enjoyment of his class and students. But no, it was back to business as usual, and the daily grind of the prof and his students, the king and his subjects, the CEO and his subordinates.

Toward the end of the semester I happened to go to the church of one of the students I was discipling. It was a rather stuffy, formal ceremony with robes and candles and padded pews, until the 6-foot 10-inch former basketball player-turned-pastor stood to preach. Man, did he lay it on the line and everyone listened intently. At the end, he asked if anyone wanted to come forward to humble themselves before God and commit their life to Christ. But for a full, very awkward minute, no one moved.

Suddenly, I spotted across the small sanctuary a single, solitary figure walking slowly to the front, getting down on his knees, and humbling himself before God. I had to do a double and triple take to truly believe it was really Dr. Johansen there on his knees, confessing his sins and committing his heart to Christ. The music played, the pastor waited, but no one else apart from the distinguished, esteemed professor responded to the invitation to seek God's face.

At that moment, I looked into my own heart; the pride, the arrogance, the judgmental attitudes I had toward the prof and so many others. I went home that day and got on *my* face before God and confessed my own sins, seeking and receiving Christ's cleansing. I did at home—in private—what *only* Dr. Johansen was willing to do that Sunday in public. The Lord used him to show me my own self sufficiency and conceit. Looking back, all I can surmise is, he must have been…a godsend.

The Box:
What profs (or students) have impressed you with their Christian witness or Christlike character? And how?

- Crockett → says religion should be #1

- Libby → Jewish but very practicing

82

A Thing Called Love
Mocha

When you take the ingredients of cappuccino and add some sweet chocolate, you get Mocha. Some consider this to be a girl's drink, but a lot of guys order it too.

God designed male-female relationships to be healthy, enjoyable, yes even sweet. But some have turned it sour.

Love: let's jump in and see where it takes us.

Fifteen Differences
Between Guys and Girls

I BET YOU DIDN'T THINK THE LIST GUY COULD EVEN COUNT TO 15. I'm not trying to brag, but you need to know that I graduated in the *top* 75% of my high school class. I'm telling you, you're dealing with a being of superior intelligence here. I'm also seeing how my academic accomplishments have impacted my character. Thus, my next book may well be entitled *"Humility—And How I Attained It."* Stay tuned!

My facetious opening paragraph demonstrates one of the differences between guys and girls I've noticed over the years. Many of us guys sometimes think it is a little uncool to study hard and make good grades, but all the while try to impress others as to just how brilliant we truly are. On the other hand, most of the girls I've known seem to be faithful to attend class, complete assignments, and pursue excellence in their studies. But they also feel no compulsion to flaunt their grade point average to us slackers! Those were the girls who were walking the walk, while we were just talking the talk.

I know there are a multitude of exceptions, even in the area of studies, but I want to spend a few minutes with you to explore the serious (and some not-so-serious) differences between guys and girls, men and women, gentlemen and ladies—plug in whatever titles are most politically correct on your campus!

Knowing you are now accustomed to my high standards of careful research, I pecked out the phrase: "differences between men and women" into my search engine and came up with 442,732 responses. Now, I can't say I looked them all up, but there are some intriguing sites you might want to explore. For instance, I learned that Amazon.com offers a book written by a woman and her husband entitled: *Why Men Don't Iron: The Fascinating and Unalterable Differences Between Men and Women*. I scrolled down to glance at the readers' reviews, only to find a young man who resented the title, declaring his ironing proficiencies, and announced he was writing a book entitled: *Why All Women Authors are Stupid!* Wow. Wonder if he's married?!

After reading that rather immature version of the battle of the sexes, I find it hard to believe that anyone truly thinks there are absolutely *no* differences between guys and girls, except maybe an accidental switching of a chromosome or two. Well, read on, and tell me if you don't see a myriad of distinctions between guys and girls that goes way beyond "environmental molding" and supports the concept that we *do* have a Creator who purposely made male and female mentally, physically, psychologically, and even spiritually diverse.

Don't give me credit for this list, though. There are hundreds of these various "differences" lists floating around all over the internet with absolutely no indications of their original sources. Copy and paste any of these, plug them into your favorite search engine and see what I mean. Well, enough disclaimers. Enjoy!

1. Even though a guy has 50% more brute strength than a girl, she is able to withstand higher temperatures than he can.

2. A girl has a larger stomach, kidneys, liver, and appendix than a guy, but she has smaller lungs, thus giving her less breathing capacity than a guy.

3. A guys' right hemisphere of the brain is better developed, therefore they are more visual, mathematic, exploring, more sex oriented, and commit most violent crime. Girls, though, have the left hemisphere more developed and are therefore more verbal, communicative, sensitive, and more prone to phobias and depression.

4. Guys use restrooms solely for biological reasons—to drain their bladder. Girls, on the other hand, use restrooms as a social lounge. Guys will never speak a word or make eye contact with others they don't know there. But girls who've never even met will, by the time they're finished, leave laughing out loud together like old friends.

5. When the restaurant check comes, each of the guys will all throw big bills out on the table to supposedly pay for the tab. When the check comes for the girls, they will each get out their calculator to verify the total and what their down-to-the-penny part is.

6. All week, a girl will thoughtfully make an extensive list of things to purchase at the store and when she arrives, she walks directly from item to item, comparing prices and coupons. When the fridge is empty and starting to grow things, a guy will just show up at the closest store and start cruising up and down every aisle, throwing in his basket anything that looks appealing. Even though his cart is jam-packed, he will try to butt in the "10 items-or-less" checkout line.

7. A guy has five items in his bathroom—a razor, shaving cream, a bar of soap (maybe), a toothbrush, and towel from Holiday Inn. The average number of items in a typical girl's bathroom is reported to be as high as 437, the majority of which a guy could not even tell what they are or are used for.

8. When a girl says she will be ready in five minutes, she's using the same meaning of time as when a guy says the football game has *just* five minutes left to play. Neither the guy or girl is counting time outs, commercials, or replays!

9. A girl believes that visitors will be impressed by a clean house. A guy believes the visitors will be impressed by his large stereo.

10. Guys don't decorate their handwriting, they just chicken-scratch. Girls will pull out their scented, color coordinated stationary and use ridiculously large circles, hearts, and loops to finish off their i's, p's, and g's. It is a real hassle to read a letter from a girl. Even when she is *dumping* a guy, she'll finish it off with a smiley face at the end!

11. If a girl is out driving and she finds herself in unfamiliar surroundings, she will stop at a gas station and ask for directions. Guys, of course, consider this to be a sign of weakness. A guy will never stop and ask for directions. They will drive in a circle for hours, all the while saying things like, "Looks like I've found a new way to get there," and, "I know I'm in the neighborhood. I recognize that Home Depot store."

12. With the exception of female bodybuilders who call each other names like "Ultimate Pecs" and "Big Turk," women disdain the use of nicknames. If Amber, Suzanne, Katherine, and Natalie get together for lunch, they will call each other Amber, Suzanne, Katherine, and Natalie. But if Mike, Dave, Rob, and Aaron go out on the town, they will affectionately refer to each other as Bullet-Head, Godzilla, Peanut-Butt, and Yard-Dart.

13. A girl worries about the future until she gets a husband, while a guy never worries about the future until he gets a wife.

14. A girl marries a guy *expecting* him to change, but he usually doesn't. A guy marries a girl thinking she will *always* be the same—and of course, she won't.

15. Girls love cats. Guys say they love cats, but when the girl isn't looking, he kicks the cat.

I could have been much more scientific and brought in the big guns like neurologist Dr. Richard Restak from Georgetown School of Medicine or psychologist Dr. Michael Conner from Oregon to prove to you that men and women differ in *every* cell of their beings. My approach, though, was to appeal to your funny bone and hope that it somehow seeps up into your brain!

Our conclusion?

Guys and girls are different.
And that's good!

Genesis 2 is where it all began.

> "Then the Lord God formed man of dust from the ground, and breathed into his nostrils the breath of life; and man became a living being." (Genesis 2:7)

> "Then the Lord God said, "It is not good for the man to be alone; I will make him a helper suitable for him." (Genesis 2:18)

> "The Lord God fashioned into a woman the rib which He had taken from the man, and brought her to the man." (Genesis 2:22)

Even though our fulfillment in life can ultimately be found in God alone, He has designed the two genders to *complete* each other—not to *compete* with each other. They are definitely equal, but certainly different—in almost every area of life. Just for fun, I would like to throw in one final "bonus list" to help you identify whether you are currently a "competer" or a "completer" in how you relate to the opposite sex. Are you an:

1. **Eliminator**—these people deny there are any differences at all. They will demand and manipulate the other gender to see it *their* way.

2. **Accommodator**—these people deep down *know* there are differences, but choose to ignore them. They are in denial and seek to avoid understanding the opposite sex at every turn.

3. **Appreciator**—these people are beginning to see the diversity as *necessary* to healthy relationships, realizing that God uses the differences to mature and grow them.

4. **Celebrator**—these people have embraced the differences and actually enjoy them. They see how they can fit in and complement the other gender. They view the sharp contrasts of mind, will, and emotion as pluses, not minuses.

Which of these four categories would you currently place yourself? Wherever you are on the spectrum, keep moving downward, would you? If you will give up your independence and determine to be a team player, you can move from an "eliminator" to a "celebrator." I promise it will aid you in becoming a wise, balanced guy or girl who is in for one rare, but fulfilling, marriage some day.

Guys and girls are different!
Can you hear me now?

The Box:
What are some other differences you have observed over the years?

- a lack of gratitude
- care about you initially, then move to friends

Six Steps to Dynamite Dating:
Going Against the Grain of Your Culture

I CAN REMEMBER IT LIKE IT WAS YESTERDAY. I WAS A freshman in love! Yes, I was a Christian as was she, but our emotions were more wrapped up in one other than in Jesus Christ. I had this gnawing feeling the Lord wanted us to break up, but I wouldn't listen. Most of my Christian buddies had girlfriends, and certainly all my fraternity brothers did. Why shouldn't I? I carried this heavy load of rationalization around with me through the fall semester. She and I finally got enough courage to bring up the subject, talk and make a decision. Using our head and not just our heart, we broke up because we felt it was God's will.

That night I went and hid in a dark, empty classroom and cried for three hours. Not because I felt sad or jilted, but because 100 pound weights had been taken off my shoulders! I'm not very emotional, but that night there was a steady stream of joyous tears signaling I was finally free! Having fully obeyed, I was now willing to do *anything* and *everything* God wanted me to. This gave me the courage to make another important decision that night. For the rest of my college years, I resolved I would develop *friendships* with other Christian girls, *not* romances. Making a commitment like this may sound radical and unrealistic to some, but for me, it was a choice that allowed me to develop the personal and spiritual foundation I would need to last a lifetime.

Spending those college years building genuine brother-sister relationships with girls, along with studying the Scriptures to learn what a godly relationship looked like, aided me in piecing together a Christ-honoring plan that would help me be successful in this modern day, mostly American concept we call "dating". Just because we can't find it in the Bible or in most countries around the world doesn't make it wrong, but I want to warn you, if you follow these "Six Steps to Dynamite Dating", you *will be* going against the grain of your culture. But, rest assured, you will also be pleasing to God and preparing yourself for an awesome marriage someday. And now for the list!

Step #1: Date only committed Christians

"You will marry *someone* that you date" may be one of the few original things I've ever uttered. It's so obvious that it's humorous, but still our country, where we get to *choose* our mates, has one of the highest divorce rates in the world. If someday you want a Christ centered marriage (which clearly requires the commitment of two Christ centered people), then you better start with the end in mind and take a close look at whom you're attracted to. Yes, I do believe 2 Corinthians 6:14, which says, "Do not be yoked together with unbelievers," means not to marry non-Christians, but if I were you, I'd set my sights on dating and marrying someone who is more than *just* a believer.

The key is to build opposite sex friendships with other committed Christians who have a vision and passion for following Christ, for becoming like Christ and for reaching out to others with the gospel. The only *real* way for you to know if these values will be true of them in the future is to look at their past. Check out their track record to see if their talk matches their walk, recognizing that college students are notorious for changing and adapting their goals to line up with their latest flame!

Step #2: Plan your dates in advance

Having the same goals is one of the essentials for any strong dating or marriage relationship. Not only does it take time (i.e. years) to develop and live out those goals, it takes careful planning too. Bill Gothard, founder of *Basic Youth Conflicts* seminars, says "the chief purpose of dating is to achieve spiritual oneness." If you incorporate that purpose into your dating life, it will require you to prayerfully map out your activities, helping you and your date draw closer to God through your time together. This approach is a rarity in this age of "entertainment addicted" Christians where most couples seem to always end up at the local movie theater, or the couch—watching another late night video rental!

I'd like to talk to the guys right now, because I believe you are primarily responsible for the spiritual leadership in a relationship. Cultivate you and your date's love for God, for the Scriptures and for others by planning out enjoyable, but meaningful activities that produces fulfillment and mutual respect for each other. If your dating style is just kind of a lazy "hanging out", consider transforming yourself into "the man with the plan!" If you come up with the what, when, where and how, it will not only communicate that you care enough to do some advanced thinking, but she will respect you as a spiritual leader who knows where he's going!

Step #3: Save yourself for marriage

Here's the vicious cycle that many college couples go through each weekend:

First of all, he *calls up*,
then of course, they must *dress up*,
he then drives over to *pick up*,
fully stocked to *drink up*,
only to eventually *throw up*,
but still later that night choosing to *shack up*,
and with a headache the next morning they finally *wake up*,
once again possessing a deep nagging feeling they've really *messed up*!

I hate to break the news to my female readers, but many college guys show love to a girl in order to obtain "sexual access". But in the same way guys give love to get sex, there are an equal number of girls who are guilty of giving sex in order to get love. Our holy God, who thought up sex, didn't say "Let the marriage bed be undefiled" in Hebrews 13:4 to rob us of physical pleasure, but instead to give it to us in fullness, and at the right time. In my counseling over the years, I've observed that the degree to which a couple is sexually intimate *before* marrying is the same degree they lack sexual satisfaction *after*. Read and talk through one of the excellent Christian books out on dating and marriage. It will help you set up and stick to Biblical standards, build trust, and prepare you someday to have one romantic marriage!

Step #4: Work on communication

If you're dating someone who wants a little less talk and a lot more "action", you might want to check their spiritual pulse. Getting to know a person's body has nothing to do with getting to know the person inside that body. In fact, communication vanishes as the fog of guilt rolls in. *Anybody* can kiss, but how about carry on a meaningful conversation? In other words, if you end up marrying the person you're dating, the wedding night may be great, but what do you talk about at breakfast the next morning?! And as the years slip by, our beautiful bodies have a way of sagging and wrinkling, so there better be a deep bond of friendship that outlasts temporal physical attraction.

Learn how to ask good questions, how to share facts *and* feelings, and how to listen. There may be a reason God gave us two ears and only one mouth! Get to know their past and present, likes and dislikes, strengths and weaknesses, values and dreams. Most married couples are shocked when they realize 90% of their dating period was activities and only 10% communication, and that after the honeymoon, those percentages reversed themselves! Understand God made men and women with a spirit, soul and body, then later handed us divine instructions on how to connect with one another, in *that* order.

Step #5: Throw out expectations

Sometimes pressure comes from within when one partner has stronger feelings than the other and wants to always *define the relationship* (i.e. a DTR talk). Jealousy and possessiveness dominate many couples, and the only brand of relationships some students know are the conditional kind that always says, "I'll love you if..." or "I love you because..." Give each other lots of room to roam, earnestly desiring God's best for *them* even if it's not you! And why let your heart be torn in half every time there's a breakup? Let's face it, *every* dating relationship you get into is going to end until the "right one" comes along. Relax, go slow, build a friendship, and beware of someone who, on your first date, peppers you with questions about how many children you want!

Pressure sometimes comes from others who are flashing their engagement rings everywhere or asking not so subtle questions like, "When are you two going to tie the knot?" or "Aren't you going out this weekend?" *Having* to go on a date each Friday or Saturday night is a sign of insecurity and discontentment. Refuse to allow others to rope you into a dating pattern or relationship that you're uncomfortable with. Having been in thirteen weddings before I got married, it's a miracle I was able to withstand my friends' joking and jabbing until age 28 (my wife to be was almost 27) when we finally walked the aisle. Take your time and don't force it. Let *God* develop the feelings in both of your hearts, in His way and in His timing.

Step #6: Focus on becoming the right person

Looking for love in all the wrong places, students are frantically turning to internet dating, matchmaking services, even want ads in their search for intimacy. The guys have replaced wife swapping with wife shopping, while many females come to college to get their MRS degree and, if they're not engaged by Christmas of their senior year, hit the panic button big time! But if you'll focus on *becoming* the right person,* instead of *finding* the right person, the Lord will bring along someone that far surpasses your little checklist.

Are you willing to spend your college years (and maybe beyond) preparing to do it God's way, instead of the world's way? You better, because statistics show that 72% of couples divorce if one partner is less than 21, and if one of the partners is 26 or less, there's a 55% chance they'll be split up before their fifth anniversary. I've had couples tell me, "You don't understand, *we're* different. We're *really* in love!" so many times I could gag. Truly, the riskiest decision you'll ever make is who you'll marry, and if this is true, then *who* you date, and *how* you date, can make you or break you.

A final truth that transcends any list is the fact that *no* human relationship can fill our deepest needs to love and be loved. Jesus Christ *alone* fits into the God shaped vacuum in each of us. Dating, even marriage will turn out to be a cheap anesthetic for an empty life until we are *totally* satisfied in Him and can pray Psalm 73:25 back to the only *true* lover of our soul:

> "Whom have I in heaven but Thee,
> and besides Thee, I desire nothing on earth."

The Box:
Which of the six steps do you need to work on? How so?

---

*You can do this by being a Matthew 6:33 person and staying on the right road by seeking the Kingdom of God and His righteousness first.

Four Scenes from a Gay Lover

Scene #1: Brent

BRENT WAS ONE OF MY ROOMMATES IN COLLEGE. YES, HE was different, but delightful all the same. He was meticulous in the way he dressed, cooked, cleaned, in *every* single area of his life. Brent never told us he was gay, but as time wore on, the other room mates (and myself) wondered. When he graduated he developed a successful career and I kept up with him off and on until one day I received word, totally unexpected, that he had died—of AIDS.

I never had the courage to ask Brent about his sexual preference or whether or not he was allowing Jesus Christ to control that part of his life along with the other areas. Brent was a private person, his almost abrupt form of politeness keeping all who would seek to go deeper with him at arm's length. But, why didn't I attempt to dig deeper? Why didn't I try to reach out and help? I now regret not caring enough to ask the tough questions, to listen, to pray, to really, truly love.

Scene #2: Kendall

Late one night I was asked to come counsel with a young man who was involved in our college ministry. Never in my life had I seen a person more tormented or deluged with demonic attacks than this fellow believer. Kendall asked to see me so he could confess his homosexual thought life and behavior and plead for help from his bondage. But all I could do was sit and pray and hurt with him. You see, he had made a series of choices that had devastating consequences. What started out as a thought became an action, and that action became a habit, and that habit had turned into a stronghold. And strongholds don't let go easily.

Tears do not come easily for me. I don't know if it's a product of my "objective personality" or a sometimes stone-cold heart. I certainly cannot manufacture tears. But that night, I could not help myself. Even though I couldn't really identify with Kendall's struggle, I was face to face with a young man in absolute agony. And so, I literally cried out to God for freedom. Freedom from pain, from sin, from Satan—calling out in the name and power and blood of Jesus Christ. I know that love is a verb and I was, in my small, seemingly insignificant way, trying to put it to work.

Scene #3: Robert

As I stood to give the eulogy of one of the most successful businessmen in this huge metropolitan city, I wondered why. Why did he have to die so young? Why did he have to suffer so much at the end—his body rotting away by the hour during his final weeks on earth? Why did his faithful wife and stellar kids have to endure all the ridicule and embarrassment? Why? Well, because this man had made the choice to live an "alternate lifestyle." And the result of his choice? He had died of AIDS. And this was before the medical community really even knew what to call the plague that was ravaging the homosexuals in our country. This successful jet-setter had gotten bored with the normal and wanted to experiment with the abnormal. God's plan to meet our sexual needs no longer satisfied him. He was looking for more.

Believe it or not, he was lured into this new way of life by a minister. And as I looked out over that crowd of prominent citizens, my heart broke for this man. It didn't have to end like this. The story could have—it should have—had a completely different final chapter. We all loved this man, but haunted by so many unanswered "why's?"

Scene #4: Me

I'd like to come out of the closet today. Yes, I am a gay lover. No, I am not a *gay* lover. I am a gay *lover*. There is a difference. I promise you, I am as heterosexual as they come, but I have a deep love for those who call themselves "gay". No, I am not a pastor or counselor, and I don't have any quick and easy steps to vanquish this war that rages in the hearts of thousands of men and women across our nation—and world. But let's talk about it for a minute. Some, at this point, might try to throw in the old adage: Love the sinner, but hate the sin. Isn't that just a bunch of doubletalk that some right wing televangelist came up with to justify his loathing of people different from him? That may be, but those who have children understand the concept of hating sin, but loving the person, all too well. Sometimes I downright despise something one of my teenage sons is into, but my unconditional love for him never wavers. In fact, it is my love for him that propels me to hate that which I know will destroy him!

I remember years ago when a scientific study first came out that indicated there may be a genetic reason a person becomes a homosexual. Initially, the gay community was outraged, claiming the scientists were implying they had some sort of inferior DNA or defect. But, as time wore on, more and more homosexuals began embracing this theory. Why? Because it justified their lifestyle and gave them the excuse they were looking for to turn their back on the truth.

What truth?

Romans 1:25-27

    v. 25   "For they exchanged the truth of God for a lie...."

    v. 26 "For this reason God gave them over to degrading

passions—women exchanging the natural function for the unnatural…"

v. 27 "In the same way, the men abandoned the natural function of the woman and burned in their desire for one another…."

What was the result of their choices? Verse 27 tells us these homosexuals were "men with men committing indecent acts and receiving in their own persons the due penalty of their error."

Verse 32 says that these individuals "know the ordinance of God, that those who practice such things are worthy of death, and they not only do the same, but also give hearty approval to those who practice them."

Why are some homosexuals so passionate, so vocal, so radical about getting special rights or quotas for themselves? The impression is they're looking for any shred of validation that will somehow assuage their deeply wounded and scarred consciences. This is why they not only engage in these immoral behaviors, but they also "give hearty approval to those who practice them" (v. 32).

Over the years, our family has invited several homosexual college students at different times to move in with us in order to encourage and befriend them. I have counseled all kinds of people with all kinds of struggles, but I have never in my life seen more self-inflicted agony and slavery than what I have observed in these young men. Some admit their perversion and attempt, with God's help, to conquer their sin. Others, though, spend a lifetime attempting to rationalize their choices. I have, and always will, love these men, especially one student who also later died of AIDS.

I guess I'm old enough to observe a subtle, but tragic, evolution our culture has gone through over the last couple of decades. There was a time when our various leaders (and even the media) would refer to male and female homosexual activities as unlawful, even sinful. Then I noticed a gradual shift where our society came to accept the gay values as *normal*. Finally, now it seems as if TV, movies, newspapers, magazines, (even some denominations!) are unashamedly flaunting it, almost daring us to dispute the rightness of their way of life. For years now, and without even realizing it, most people have actually been *paying* their regular cable and movie rental fees to these groups who've slowly (but purposely) been moving us from *condemnation* to *toleration*, to now *celebration* of the homosexual agenda.

When and how (and more importantly why) did we switch the price tags and place a higher premium on tolerance over truth? But as humans we don't get to define truth, do we? God has already done that for us and, again, *we* don't break God's laws...they break us! You see, I have a struggle too. I have to choose every day whether I will follow what God says is right or the "politically correct" peer pressure our culture puts on all of us. No one can escape the fact that God says He abhors homosexuality and has proclaimed it to be the bottom of the barrel of a downward spiral of sin and corruption. Over the centuries, many a great civilization has been destroyed not from without, but within, as indecency and degeneration finally ripped a gaping hole in the moral fabric of that society.

With all my pontifications, I'm starting to sound like a TV preacher, aren't I? But I promise not to ask you to send me any donations! I just think God has put into each of us a sense of right and wrong and I don't want any of us to call right what *God* says is wrong. You might be wondering what it is I am asking you to do with all this information. Well, I would like to issue you an invitation today.

Will you join me as a gay *lover* too?

Yes, I want you to acknowledge the truth of what God clearly states about homosexuality, but at the same time reach out in compassion to the men and women who are in desperate need to know—and experience—the absolute, unconditional love of Jesus Christ.

The Box:

Do you know anyone who says they are gay? If so, what are some ways you can show Christ's love (even tough love!) to them?

not seems to unfair

Going Deep
Breve

Made with beans from the mountains of South America or Indonesia (maybe Java?) this coffee drink is made with thicker milk—almost cream. An inexperienced barista may look at you cock-eyed when placing your order. Fear not, that just means you are "in the know."

The mature believer knows what they want, knows where they're going and is willing to pay a price to get there.

How about you? Ready to go deep?

Four Exit Ramps
You *Don't* Want to Take!

IT WAS MIDNIGHT ON SAN FRANCISCO'S GOLDEN GATE Bridge when my eleven-year-old Volvo died and stopped right in the middle lane. I could see my beautiful wife and nine month old daughter at my side—but nothing else. You see, the fog was so thick we could barely make out other cars, much less the bridge or the bay. Suddenly, out of nowhere, a booming voice spoke to us, "PUT YOUR VEHICLE IN NEUTRAL." I immediately looked up, thinking maybe I was getting a heavenly revelation. Coming to my senses, I then glanced in my rear view mirror, only to see a giant truck with tires attached to its front bumpers about to start pushing us. It's job was to keep the bridge clear of *any* obstructions, and it continued to propel us forward (its only stop was to allow me to pay the toll, of course) with increasing speed.

Now, off the bridge, I had no idea where the driver was directing us. "VEER RIGHT!" the microphoned voice bellowed again, and I could see he was pushing us off onto an exit ramp and up a narrow, winding, deserted road with a drop off that is giving me sweaty palms right now, even as I write about it. After about 300 yards, he stopped, turned around and disappeared back to the highway and the bridge. So, there we were—all alone—past midnight now, on a pitch-black moonless evening without even as much as a flashlight or matches to help me attempt to find the problem with our lifeless Volvo.

"Oh God," I prayed silently, so as not to alarm my wife or wake our sleeping baby, "I need Your help right now!" I felt like I was exposing my family to one of the most lonely, isolated, and dangerous places on the planet. And it was *my* fault we took this exit ramp to nowhere.

"Why did I not service my car before we left?" I thought.

"Why did I allow that guy to push us all the way out here into never-never land?" I asked myself.

"How in the world can we get back to the main road—and to safety?" I wondered.

How about you? Have you ever taken a wrong exit ramp in your life? Whether it was of your own doing, or you allowed someone—or some thing—to do the pushing? Have you ever found yourself *out* of God's will, wandering around in the wilderness, coming face to face with temptations and trials you *never* thought would come your way?

Welcome to the real world.

Getting on and staying on God's road is one of the greatest challenges we face as followers of Jesus Christ. Allowing Satan, the world, or our own flesh to get us off track *might* just be a temporary detour, but it could mean…total destruction! Look how Peter warns us in 1 Peter 5:8:

> *"Be of sober spirit, be on the alert. Your adversary, the devil, prowls about like a roaring lion, seeking someone to devour."*

The enemy's goal is not just to distract or disrupt us, but to DEVOUR us! I'm not trying to frighten you (too much) but if you take one of the four exit ramps I describe, you could end up *being* the main course at one of Satan's late night dinner parties.

Exit ramp #1: Fear

In his excellent book, *When Fear Seems Overwhelming*, Dr. Larry Crabb notes that we live our lives based on fear. We do the things that are safe and comfortable for us, and we avoid (or run from) things that frighten or intimidate us. I once thought courage was the absence of fear. Not so. In fact, someone interviewed the still-living congressional medal of honor winners (the medal that says "VALOR" on it) and asked them what their definition of courage was. All of them, in one form or another, said that courage isn't the absence of fear—it's *doing* what you're afraid to do.

Whether it's WWII facing the Nazis at Normandy beach or trusting God with our future, we must walk *toward* our fears. Easy to say, hard to do, but letting the fear of what others think of us, the fear of the lordship of Christ, or the fear of earthly dangers control us can be exit ramps we *don't* want to take. Paul challenged Timothy, his young disciple, saying,

> "For God has not given us a spirit of fear, but of power and love and sound mind." (2 Timothy 1:7)

If God has given us everything we need for victory, why are we still relying on our own puny little resources? The real issue is not how to escape our fears, but how to handle them. And we can—if we will stay on God's road with our eyes fixed on Him.

Exit ramp #2: Pride

As a cocky young freshman, I was walking along one day with the upperclassman who was attempting to help me spiritually. Impressed by how many students I was influencing for Christ, I subtly boasted, "Terry, I'm really struggling with pride." He stopped, looked at me, and shot back, "What do *you* have to be proud about?" Having my arrogance totally exposed, I stuttered and stammered, "I guess nothing."

You see, I was focused on building up *my* little kingdom, of building a name for *my*self, of stealing glory from the *only* One who deserved it: "I am the Lord, that is My name. I will not give My glory to another…" Isaiah 42:8 teaches. The marks of pride are usually evident to everyone—except ourselves! It raises its ugly head in the forms of defensiveness, prayerlessness, comparison, and lack of teachability.

One question you can ask yourself: Can you follow well? You'll never be a great leader until you learn how to be a great follower. For instance, if you don't have someone discipling you, it's probably because you don't *want* someone discipling you! If so, decide now to turn in your "Loners for Christ" club membership, humble yourself before God, find someone who has been on God's road for a while and start to follow and learn from them. You'll be glad you did!

Exit ramp #3: Immorality

I believe sexual sins leave the deepest scars in people's lives. We can be forgiven of *any* evil doing, but, for some reason, it's almost impossible for us to forget these "sins of the flesh" that seem to be seared into our conscience for many years to come. Whether its pre-marital sexual involvement or the cheap substitutes we find in a lot of TV, movies and romance novels, they rob us of our purity, self esteem, and worst of all—fellowship with the Lord.

2 Corinthians 10:4,5 tells us Satan is using all of his resources to influence and control our minds. The solution, Paul says, is to saturate ourselves with the Word, seeking to "bring every thought captive to the obedience of Christ." This is especially tough for guys because we are *so* stimulated by what we see. Now that the internet is so accessible, the enemy can push a young student toward this exit ramp with the mere click of a mouse. Images will instantly appear that can be forever stored in the back of our brain's hard drive, producing a spiritual virus with potentially devastating long-term effects to our life and marriage.

Remember, we are just temporarily passing through this life and as you traverse this "highway to heaven" the Lord has you on, be careful what you look at, what you think about, and what you touch. Yes, God does love you and has a wonderful plan for your life. Stay true to Him and you will get to fully experience it.

Exit ramp #4: Bitterness

As I was graduating from college, I was burned big time by a landlord who chose to keep our security deposit—even though we had left her rental house in immaculate shape. Frustration turned into anger, anger into resentment, and resentment into a deep seated, severely entrenched…bitterness.

I had been wronged and the fury swelling inside of me had started to permeate every hour of my day, every conversation I had, every relationship in my world. The writer of Hebrews 12:15 described *me* when he said,

> "See to it that no ones come short of the grace of God;
> that no root of bitterness springing up cause trouble,
> and by it many be defiled."

I was not able to accept, nor extend, the grace of God and, as a result, I was not only poisoning myself, but everyone around me as well.

Of the four exit ramps I've described, I believe this is the hardest one to come back from. The far reaching tentacles of this "root of bitterness" can *so* engulf our soul that it seems nothing can break its grip. It may not be a confiscated security deposit that rattles your cage, but when you get bitter over another person's unfaithfulness, betrayal, or slander, the one it *most* destroys is staring back at you in the mirror. Take a long look and determine to extend the same grace to others the Lord so lavishly poured out upon you.

Oh, I almost forgot. Do you wanna' know the end of the Golden Gate/dead car/lonely exit story? Desperate, I squinted hard and could see the far away parking lot lights of the maintenance building next to the bridge at the bottom of the exit ramp. So I pushed the Volvo around, put it in neutral, and, by faith, coasted all the way down (with no headlights or power steering), hoping I would not run into anyone or anything on the way. Relieved to finally roll it into the brightly lit parking lot, guess who drives up, but the truck driver with the booming voice and front bumper tires! He kindly got out, gave us a jump, and sent us on our way. Not such a bad guy, after all! I then breathed a prayer of thanks, compliments of old timer country singer Willie Nelson:

On the road again.
I just can't wait to get on the road again.

The Box:
What are the "exit ramps" you have been tempted to take over the years? How can you guard against each?

"Only the Lonely"
Four Songs that Sing the Blues
(And How You Can Beat Them!)

SCROLLING THROUGH THE MUSIC ARCHIVES, WE COME UPON the man of mystery, rock and roller Roy Orbison. With his jet black shades to match his jet black hair, he was popular for more than just his hit song, "Pretty Woman." Before the award winning movie came out, named after Orbison's song, most believed his 1960 chart topper "Only the Lonely" was his greatest work. Now, in the quiet of my own office, pecking away on the old laptop, I'm trying to stimulate *my* creative juices by looping this "goldie-oldie" over and over again. His deep baritone voice crooning:

> *Only the lonely know how I feel tonight.*
> *Only the lonely know this feeling ain't right.*
>
> *Only the lonely know why I cry. Only the lonely.*
>
> *Maybe tomorrow, a new romance.*
> *No more sorrow, but that's the chance.*
>
> *Only the lonely know why I cry. Only the lonely.*

As wealthy and famous as Orbison was, many of his songs seemed to have a dark and forlorn feel to them, seeming to reflect the pain in his own life. Born in a small Texas town in 1936 and dying of a heart attack in 1988, Orbison was acquainted with grief, having lost his wife and two sons in a two-year period, and with a career described, at best, as up and down.

Even the fun, uptempo song "Pretty Woman" speaks of his isolation. Let me crank it up a bit and let you in on a few of the lyrics:

Pretty woman, walkin' down the street.
Pretty woman, the kind I'd like to meet.

Are you lonely just like me?

Pretty woman, stop for a while.
Pretty woman, talk for a while.

Are you lonely just like me?

Pretty woman, don't walk on by.
Pretty woman, don't make me cry.

Are you lonely just like me?

Orbison wasn't the only artist to sing of his feelings of rejection and desolation. Maybe you've heard of Britney Spears or Puff Daddy (excuse me, Diddy!). They each sing a song simply named "Lonely." One of the best selling albums of all time was the Beatles "Sergeant Peppers Lonely Hearts Club Band." If you search really hard, I bet you could find that 33 rpm piece of plastic antiquity somewhere in your parent's attic!

Let's get current for a minute:

A recent Grammy Awards song of the year was *Boulevard of Broken Dreams* sung by Green Day. Even though the fame and fortune is coming at them at high speed, their chorus cries out "I walk alone. I walk alone."

Akon is from Senegal, but owns diamond mines in South Africa. His impressive voice matches up nicely with his orange Lamborghini Gallardo sports car. So, with all this, why was his recent number one hit once again entitled— you guessed it—"*Lonely*"? He repeats over and over: "I'm so lonely, I'm Mr. Lonely. I have nobody." Wow...

Due to his phenomenal success, fellow rapper Snoop Dogg calls Eminen the "great white American hope." But all hope seems to have slipped away as Eminen raps: "In between the silence, living is an empty space...I just don't wanna be lonely."

Why do I dwell so much on this one *lonely* topic? Aren't there other issues that face mankind besides this single, solitary struggle I speak of? Of course, but this is a biggie. How big? Nobel Peace Prize winner Mother Theresa, a famous Catholic nun who rescued the dying in India, was asked toward the end of her life of sacrifice and service, "What is the greatest human tragedy?" Expecting her to say "poverty" or "disease" or "lack of love", she quietly uttered one word: "Loneliness."

Loneliness? How could anyone be lonely with a world of almost seven billion people surrounding us night and day? Even though 6,279 people die each *hour*, 15,020 are being added. Hey, let's party! That nets out to 8,741 new friends *every single hour!* Loneliness seems like the last emotion we would experience with a wall to wall world of billions of people. The reason, of course, is because we've *all* put walls up. Two-way walls that keep everyone out and keep us in; safe and toasty and…lonely.

In my short life, I've come to realize that many times the loneliest people are the ones who seem to have it all. Maybe they got to the top of the ladder and realized all the trappings of this life didn't really satisfy them like they thought they would. The rest of us are still in the elusive search of fame, wealth and happiness. Will we be disappointed too if and when we achieve our dreams of a "perfect life"?

Many of today's college students are determined to defy the odds. Deep down you might suspect that money doesn't bring happiness, but why not give it a try? In fact, a whopping 52% of students think they'll be millionaires *before* they reach the age of forty! Another 19% think it will happen after age forty, while almost a third of students (29%) have already given up hope it will ever happen. These statistics are taken from UCLA's annual survey of hundreds of thousands of entering freshmen each year across the country. The polling also revealed what percentage of those surveyed thought one of the objectives listed below was "very important" to them:

1. Being very well off financially   73.4%
2. Raising a family   73.1%

3. Helping others   61.7%
4. Owning a successful business   39.3%
5. Cleaning up the environment   17.5%

It appears that most college students' (and probably most Americans') highest achievement in life is to be "very well off financially." Maybe money will buy us friends and friends will buy us happiness. Besides, doesn't Proverbs 19:4 teach us that "wealth brings many friends, but a poor man's friend deserts him." But will lots of cold, hard cash drive away the gnawing emptiness in our souls? Will the vacuum be filled when we've acquired all the comforts and conveniences we've always fantasized about? In my day, it was summed up in the bumper sticker that read, "He who dies with the most toys wins." If the acquiring of material things beyond our wildest dreams doesn't defeat loneliness, then what does?

Hey, enough questions, statistics, and Bible verses. Let's get back to the tunes! Certainly, a rock and roll history lesson from "The King" would come in handy right now. Let me pump up the volume so we can listen in on "Heartbreak Hotel" by Elvis Presley.

Well, since my baby left me,
I found a new place to dwell.
It's down at the end of Lonely Street
at Heartbreak Hotel.

You make me so lonely baby,
I get so lonely,
I get so lonely I could die.

And although it's always crowded,
you still can find some room.
where broken hearted lovers
do cry away their gloom.

You make me so lonely baby,
I get so lonely,
I get so lonely I could die.

Hey now, if your baby leaves you,
and you got a tale to tell.

Just take a walk down Lonely Street
to Heartbreak Hotel.

Only six weeks before the death of Elvis Presley a reporter asked, "Mr. Presley, you said earlier in your life that you wanted to obtain wealth, fame, and happiness. Did you?" The king glanced at him and wistfully looked away and said, "The first two, yes. But the last? I'm lonely." Lonely! How could that be? He was surrounded by waves of adoring fans wherever he went. He could have anything or anyone he wanted. The same with Earnest Hemingway, Marilyn Monroe, even Kurt Cobain. They all sought and gained money, pleasure, even legend status from this world, but it didn't satisfy them. All three, like Elvis, took their own life. What could be the source of their loneliness? For them contentment turned out to be like a mirage in the desert, ever searching for something they would never attain.

The fourth (and final) song I'll pull lyrics from is a sad ballad that Elvis sang to his swooning fans entitled "Are You Lonesome Tonight?" Join with me as I sway to the sweet melody of his soothing voice…

Are you lonesome tonight?

Do the chairs in your parlor seem empty and bare?

Is your heart filled with pain?

The world's a stage and each must play a part.

Now the stage is bare, and I'm standing there, with emptiness all around.

If you won't come back to me, then they can bring the curtain down.

Sure enough, at age 42, this heart throb of America, from little Tupelo, Mississippi, was dead. Instead of allowing his Creator to "bring the curtain down", he chose to end the play himself. His pain had driven him from loneliness to depression, and finally to death.

Dr. Frank Minrith, a psychologist, author, and seminary professor, spent years studying people who were struggling with loneliness and depression.

He claimed the two were tied together, and as a result, gave us a definition of depression as simply: "a lack of intimacy with God and/or others." I think he's right. You see, at one point in my life, I was incredibly depressed. I was under tremendous stress, but it wasn't the anxiety that pulled me under. It was the fact that I didn't have anyone to share my pain with. I was lonely. And loneliness many times leads to depression.

I'm wondering. Are you lonely tonight? If you are, it might be because of:

**Lack of intimacy with God
and/or
lack of intimacy with others.**

The opposite of loneliness is intimacy. In fact, I believe the solution to loneliness *is* intimacy.

**Intimacy through a personal relationship with Jesus Christ.
Intimacy through personal relationships with others.**

A wealthy lawyer confronted Jesus, quizzing him as to what the greatest commandment was. You know what Jesus said: "Love the Lord your God with all your heart and with all your soul and with all your mind. This is the first and greatest commandment. And the second is like it: Love your neighbor as yourself. All the Law and the Prophets hang on these two commandments." (Matthew 22:37-39)

Breaking down the walls, opening up our hearts, and taking the risk to love are the first steps to intimacy. Seeking to love the Lord and those around us takes the focus off of ourselves. Loneliness, and even depression, can be all about *us*. Unconditionally loving God and others doesn't leave time or energy for pity parties.

One person who modeled the Great Commandment went to be with his Great Commander a few years ago. Spike White was the grand patriarch of Kanakuk, the world's largest camp, nestled around the waterways of southern Missouri. He laid down his life for thousands of kids, parents, and counselors for almost 50 years. There wasn't a selfish, "me-centered" bone in his body. Spike lived out the famous talk he would give every term to every camper entitled "God First, Others Second, and I'm Third."

Yeah, I'm sure Spike heard Orbison and Presley sing the blues of "Only the Lonely", "Pretty Woman", "Heartbreak Hotel", and "Are You Lonely Tonight?", but he was too busy following Christ by reaching out to "the lonely" of this world to worry about who loved him and who didn't. Spike wouldn't allow a big funeral service where prominent luminaries would gather to say nice things about him. Instead, he simply wanted his wife, sons, grand children, great-grandchildren and thousands like you and me to carry on his legacy of love.

Wrinkled up, sparkly-eyed, work horse of a man, Spike White was a happy, fulfilled child of God even though he didn't care a whit about obtaining riches or reputation. Instead, he chose a higher calling and understood that loneliness is simply a by product of ignoring intimacy and pursuing the wrong things in life.

How about you? Are you lonely tonight? Loneliness can end and intimacy begin for you, right now. Forget about yourself, start pouring your heart, soul, and mind into loving God and those people He has placed around you. Your life will be so full, there will be no time to sing the blues. You'll just have to leave that for Roy, Elvis, and "only the lonely."

The Box:
Have you struggled with loneliness or depression? What are some specific ways you could increase your intimacy with God and/or others?

Three Stories of
Faith and Courage

Story #1: The daring millionaire

IN 1904 YOUNG WILLIAM BORDEN GRADUATED FROM A HIGH school in Chicago. As heir to the Borden Dairy fortune, he was already worth millions. As a graduation present, his parents gave the 16-year-old Borden a trip to sail around the world. As he traveled through Europe, the Middle East, and Asia, he sensed a growing burden to reach the lost in nations cut off from the gospel. Finally, Borden wrote home to his parents, expressing, "I'm going to give my life to prepare for the mission field." One of his friends was completely shocked, letting Borden know he felt he was "throwing himself away as a missionary." When Borden heard that, he wrote two words in the front of his Bible:

"No reserves."

Even though Borden was fabulously wealthy, he arrived at Yale University in 1905 attempting to appear like any other freshman student. But soon, his classmates noticed something unique about Borden. One of them wrote: "He came to college far ahead, spiritually, of any of us. He had already given his heart in full surrender to Christ. We learned to lean on him and find in him a strength that was solid as a rock, just because of this settled purpose and consecration." An entry in Borden's journal explained what the other students were seeing in his life. It simply said:

> "Say 'no' to self and 'yes' to *Jesus* every time."

During his first year at Yale, Borden started something that impacted the entire campus for Christ. He challenged a friend to pray with him before breakfast each day, and soon a second joined them, and a third, and a fourth, and others. One of the participants explained, "William would read to us from the Bible, show us something that God had promised, and then proceed to claim the promise with assurance." By the end of his first year, 150 freshmen were meeting for prayer and Bible study each week in small groups. By the time Borden was a senior, 1000 of Yale's 1,300 students were gathering every week for this purpose. He had divided the classes up into smaller groups and assigned key student leaders to reach out and witness to a certain number, with a goal of extending salvation to every student. Borden and his leaders would go over every name and ask, "Who will take this student?" When the name of a hardened or "incorrigible" student came up and no one wanted to take them on, Borden would chime in by saying, "Put him down to me." Young Borden's ministry extended beyond Yale, as he sought to help widows, orphans, cripples, and drunks in the area, forming the Yale Hope Mission.

Borden felt the missionary call to reach out to one of the hardest to reach people groups of all, the Muslim Kansu in China. Once that goal was in sight, Borden never questioned his destiny and consistently challenged his classmates to consider missionary service, even hosting a huge student missionary conference at Yale. Even though Borden was very involved on campus and served as President of Phi Beta Kappa there at Yale, he chose not to join a fraternity. One student said, "Although he was a millionaire, William seemed to realize always that he must be about his Father's business, and not wasting time in the pursuit of amusement." He never even owned an automobile, and when others asked why, he would casually respond, "Because I can't afford one." But during his undergraduate years at Yale he gave away hundreds of thousands of dollars to Christian ministries. Once he graduated, Borden turned down several lucrative career opportunities. After one especially tempting job offer, he went home and wrote two more words in his Bible:

"No retreats."

Borden instead went on to complete a masters degree at Princeton Seminary, and then newspapers across the nation published articles about this young millionaire who raised his own support to go to China as a missionary. It was 1913 and the entire country was fascinated by this wealthy and gifted young man who turned his back on affluence and comfort in America to risk everything and go to China. On his way there, he stopped first in Cairo, Egypt, to study Arabic because he was going to be reaching out to Muslims in China. While there, he contracted spinal meningitis and died a few weeks later in a hospital room—all alone.

When news was cabled back to America that 25-year-old William Whiting Borden was dead, "a wave of sorrow went round the world." His biographer later wrote, "Borden not only *gave* away his wealth, but himself, in a way so joyous and natural that it seemed a privilege rather than a sacrifice." Many people, though, thought that Borden had *thrown* his life away. He could have had everything, but instead met an untimely death, they thought, of his *own* doing. As his associates were packing up his belongings to ship them back to the states for his burial, they found his Bible next to his hospital bed. In the front cover, underneath the words "No reserves" and "No retreats," they were astonished to see the dying Borden had also scrawled two final words: "No regrets."

No reserves
No retreats
No regrets

Although William Borden's life appeared to end prematurely, he had accomplished everything God had planned for him. In his heart of hearts the young 25-year-old millionaire missionary must have reconciled his destiny there on his death bed, making peace with God—and himself. How about you and me? There are a hundred things we could do with our lives, a hundred pursuits for which we could exchange it. But how many of them will enable you to say at the end of your life, "No reserves, no retreats, no regrets"?

Epilogue: The story of his life and early death became a rallying cry for hundreds of college students who ended up spending their lives on the mission field because of Borden of Yale.

Story #2: The loyal soldier

This well-known account of friendship and loyalty has always inspired me to never forget those whom God has brought into my life. It's the touching story of two British young men, who grew up as best friends, enlisted together and went to fight in World War I. After their training, they were assigned to serve in the same battalion, and almost immediately, were both transported to fight against the Germans in northern France. In what would turn out to be one of the bloodiest struggles in all of human history, over one million men died at the Battle of Somme in 1916. When Fred, one of the two young men, was wounded on one side of the battle field, his friend George got word from his post a distance away. After learning his lifelong buddy was lying mortally injured and stranded somewhere out in "No Man's Land" (that dangerous area separating the two armies) George had to take action.

Although his commanding officer told him not to, George immediately rushed out into No Man's Land, under heavy fire, and began searching for his friend. He frantically scoured the battle field, until finally spotting Fred. As George was dragging his unresponsive friend through the mud back to the British trenches, he himself was hit by German gunfire. A few minutes later, Fred died in George's arms, and his commanding officer walked up and scolded him for risking his life just to save someone who was destined to die anyway. George turned and looked up into the officers face and cried out, "Oh, no sir. You don't understand. I had to go! You see, when I finally reached Fred, he opened his eyes one last time, and in his final breath whispered, 'Thanks George. I *knew* that you would come.'"

There aren't many things more important than friendship, loyalty, and faithfulness. And for a human being on this planet, to have one such person to go through life with, is fortunate indeed.

Story #3: The determined explorer

Although born in Ireland, Ernest Shackleton was best known as one of England's most tenacious maritime explorers ever. As a young man he had paid his dues by serving with the merchant navy before finally getting to lead his first expeditions to Antarctica with the goal of getting to the South Pole. One of the most legendary adventures of the modern era began on August 8, 1914, when Shackleton and his crew of 27 set sail on the ship *Endurance* from England for Antarctica on what they expected to be a six-month expedition. The goal: to become the first men to traverse the frozen continent via the South Pole, an 1,800-mile journey. Before sailing, he placed ads in the London newspaper seeking to "attract" men to join them:

> *Men wanted for hazardous journey. Small wages.*
> *Bitter cold. Long months of complete darkness.*
> *Constant danger. Safe return doubtful.*
> *Honour and recognition in case of success.*

The Antarctic expedition started off fine with Shackleton and his crew having clear sailing. But, with the huge continent in plain sight, their ship, the *Endurance,* became stuck in ice and, after ten months of trying to survive and stay afloat, was eventually pounded into splinters. After he and his crew watched the *Endurance* sink into the icy sea, Shackleton took action. He built a small camp for 21 of his men on a drifting ice floe, while he and five others would attempt to sail a small, open life-boat 800 miles to South Georgia Island for help. If they could reach that island, they could launch a rescue mission back to save the rest of the crew. Miraculously, after 17 stormy days across some of the world's roughest seas, Shackleton and his team did reach South Georgia, but accidentally landed on the wrong coast. With stamina flagging, they began a 36 hour trek that took them over the island's glacier-clad mountains and into safety. Then Shackleton held true to his promise, and after two attempts, was able to finally sail back to find and save his abandoned crew—two years after the *Endurance* had set sail from England!

Not losing a single man throughout this ordeal, Shackleton's rescue turned out to be the most remarkable in maritime history. Even though he had numerous personal and moral issues in his life, Shackleton was willing to serve and lead and do anything he had to in order to help his men personally and to pull them together to accomplish a task. Sir Raymond Priestley, a famous British geologist and explorer who accompanied Shackleton on earlier Antarctic expeditions, once said, "For scientific leadership, give me Scott; for swift and efficient travel, Amundsen; but when you are in a hopeless situation, when there seems to be no way out, get on your knees and pray for Shackleton!"

"By endurance we conquer."
—Shackleton's motto

The Box:
List the top three character qualities you observed in this chapter and how you can grow in these areas.

Getting Radical
Red Eye

A cup of drip coffee with two shots of espresso in it. Also known as a *slingblade, depth charge, shot in the dark, Al Pacino, autobahn,* or *hammerhead.* Some say this is coffee "with an attitude" and is for serious java drinkers only.

Saying no to the world and yes to Jesus may sound extreme to some, but for God, it is just the "normal" Christian life.

Say goodbye to boredom. Get radical!

Five Students Who
Changed the World

WE DON'T HAVE TO LOOK FAR TO SEE THE INCREDIBLE potential of college students. Even though only one percent of the world's population is collegians, what a powerful one percent they are! This small sliver of humanity is, and will be, the leader of every facet of society. Each country sends their best and brightest to the university for education and training. Focusing your evangelistic and discipling efforts on this one percent is a *very* strategic way to expand the Kingdom of God and fulfill the Great Commission.

Almost one fourth of the world's college students reside in North America, and they represent the most reachable, recruitable, trainable, and sendable category of persons on the planet. It's true what Dr. Bill Bright of Campus Crusade said,

> "If we can win the university today,
> we will win the world tomorrow."

There is a growing openness among college students worldwide toward the gospel. Being a world and current events buff, I'm always clipping articles in newspapers about student protests and rallies in other nations. My observation is that students are more open than ever to the West, to new ideas and technology, to philosophies and beliefs that are different from their ancestors. Who and what will fill that gap? Will it be other world religions, cults, secularism, or the life-changing gospel of Jesus Christ?

The challenge, as always, is the lack of workers compared to the ripened harvest. Patti Burgin, author of *The Powerful Percent* tells of the need, "There are about 3,300 colleges in the United States. There are about 25,000 around the world. Despite the efforts of so many groups, more than a third of the world's college campuses do not have any contact with full time Christian workers." How about you? Will you step into the gap?

We're living in an amazing period of history, and as I travel to different countries, students want to meet Westerners. They want to learn English and listen to the personal, political and spiritual ideas we present. Never before has God opened the doors and hearts of so many students worldwide to allow English speaking Christians from North America to have impact. This unprecedented opportunity for sharing the gospel with students globally also brings an undeniable obligation. We have been blessed. Why? To be a blessing to others! Ecclesiastes 3:11 tells us it is *God* who has placed in us this desire to permanently impact others:

> *"God has made everything beautiful in its time,*
> *He has also set eternity in the hearts of men."*

This is especially true of college students where incredible optimism, unrestrained aspiration, and the belief that God may just be big enough to pull off what He says He will, is firmly planted in their hearts. Dennis Gaylor, National Director of Chi Alpha Campus Ministries, sees the awesome possibilities of this group as well: "College students are idealistic, energetic, and active. They comprise one of the greatest reservoirs of manpower for the cause of Jesus Christ in the entire world."

What is the potential of just one student? Throughout my years of traveling to universities around the world, I have observed that great campus revivals can usually be traced back to one person. More times than not, the spark comes from a student, not a staff person; one student who takes the person and purposes of Jesus Christ seriously.

They believe and act.

To fuel *your* vision a bit, I've chosen five students from history who, I'm sure, are in heaven's "College Student Hall of Fame."

Worldchanger #1: Ludwig Von Zinzendorf

·Born into a wealthy German family in 1700, Zinzendorf grew up and attended the University of Wittenburg to study law. At age nineteen he was looking at a painting of Christ in agony on the cross and an inscription below that read, "All this I did for you, what are you doing for Me?" From that moment on, he forsook the comfortable life of a nobleman to begin spreading the gospel throughout the world.

He started inviting Christians to come live on his farm and learn how to grow spiritually. He launched a 24-hour prayer vigil that focused on world intercession that continued unbroken for a *hundred years!* As a result, his mission society, the Moravians, sent out more missionaries the next twenty years than *all* the Protestants or Anglicans had sent out in the previous 200 years! His burning desire to reach others with the gospel issued out of his love for Christ. Asked about his passion, he replied:

"I know of only one passion; it is He and He alone."

Worldchanger #2: Samuel Mills

A tall, awkward, squeaky voiced freshman at Williams College in Massachusetts, Mills would have never been voted "Most Likely to Succeed." Because of persecution, he and four other college friends would slip out to a nearby meadow to pray and talk. On one rainy August afternoon in 1806, they were taking refuge next to a huge haystack, reading missionary biographies and interceding for the world. When the rain subsided, Mills stood up, slammed his fist into his hand, and announced,

"We can do this, if we will!"

These five young collegians stepped out in faith and not only initiated the first nationwide student movement, but also began the first six mission agencies from North America. Although there were just 25 colleges in America at the time (averaging about a hundred students each), the "Haystack Five" helped launch small world mission study and prayer clusters on many of them. Mills himself died at age 35 on a ship coming back from West Africa, having contracted malaria while setting up yet another mission agency to reach slaves on that continent.

Worldchanger #3: Lottie Moon

Lottie Moon was born and raised in a wealthy Virginia family before the Civil War. She was a well educated and cultured woman who actually measured all of four feet…three inches! Rebelling against her mother's deep-seated Baptist faith, Lottie ran off to college and ended up mocking Christians. Finally she returned to her roots after admitting, "I went to a campus revival to scoff, and came back to my room to pray all night." After graduation, passing up a marriage proposal from a prominent seminary professor was difficult, but she justified it by declaring,

> "God had first claim on my life and since the two conflicted,
> there could be no question about the result!"

Sailing for China as a single 23-year-old female missionary was unusual, but par for the course for this diminutive, but bold pioneer. At first her ministry was confined to teaching at a girl's school, but she finally struck out on her own to do evangelistic work in North China. Despite tremendous opposition, nationals did come to Christ, a church was established, and thousands were baptized over the years. But Lottie is most known for her vigorous recruiting of volunteers and money for missions. She mobilized thousands of women in the states to pray, volunteer, and enlist others to give to foreign mission work.

While she was ministering there severe drought broke out after China's "Boxer Rebellion" in 1911 and Lottie, to her own detriment, gave away *all* her money and food to help the starving Chinese. Other missionaries tried to rescue Lottie in time to save her life, loading her now frail and famished 50 lb. body on a ship headed for America. But she was too far gone and, at age 72, died on board late one December night in 1912, Christmas Eve. How appropriate that the Southern Baptist annual world missions funding effort (that has raised billions of dollars over the years) is named for Lottie Moon, and takes place at the same time each year, Christmas.

Worldchanger #4: C. T. Studd

In the early 1880's, Hudson Taylor, founder of the China Inland Mission, was back home in England recruiting workers. He interviewed several students from the distinguished Cambridge University who were burdened about how lost China's millions were. As a result, God touched the heart of C. T. Studd, a popular student from an affluent family, and the best cricket player in all of England. He and six other renowned athletes banded together and volunteered to spend their life on the mission field, giving up the fame and fortune that awaited them in professional sports.

The impact was amazing, and by the time the seven arrived in China a year later they had already recruited over 160 others to join them. God used their story to spread a wildfire of interest and decisions across the universities of the western World, and by 1900 one third of *all* foreign missionaries were ministering under the banner of the China Inland Mission. Studd lived a life of abandonment to Christ, giving away all his inheritance in order to pioneer works in China, India, and Africa. His motto?

"I'd rather run a rescue shop within a foot of hell than live within the sound of a chapel bell. If Jesus Christ be God and died for me, nothing I sacrifice is too great for Him."

Worldchanger #5: Grace Wilder

The daughter of an American missionary, Grace Wilder grew up in India. Due to her father's health, the family returned home in 1876 to live and minister near Princeton University. A few years later Grace enrolled in nearby Mount Holyoke College and promptly started a weekly Bible study for women. Before they could join, though, she required them to sign a "declaration" stating: "I hold myself willing and desirous to do the Lord's work wherever He may call me, even if it be to a foreign land." Thirty-four women signed and joined up!

Grace and her younger brother, Robert, heard about the Mt. Hermon, Massachusetts Bible conference that evangelist D. L. Moody was hosting for over 250 college men in July of 1886. Grace encouraged her brother to go and to take an even more radical version of her declaration with him to ask men to sign. This one stated,

"We the undersigned, declare ourselves willing and desirous,
God permitting, to go to the unevangelized portions of the world."

She stayed at home and prayed that 100 of the men would sign it, committing themselves to foreign missions. God answered, as exactly 100 men signed, thus launching the greatest student missions mobilization effort in history, the Student Volunteer Movement. Over the next forty years, almost 100,000 students would sign this declaration and embrace the watchword: "The Evangelization of the World in This Generation!" At age twenty-six, Grace sailed for India with her widowed mother to continue the missionary work her father began. She died in 1911, at age fifty, having given her life to mobilizing college students and evangelizing the unreached.

As I look closely at the lives of visionary men and women who have preceded us, I've concluded there are only three kinds of people on this planet:

1. Those who *watch* history
2. Those who *study* history
3. Those who *make* history

God *has* put eternity in your heart too. What are *you* going to do about it?

The Box:
Think of the kind of qualities or characteristics you are going to need to have in your life to be a "world changer." Make a list.

Five Students Who ARE
Changing the World

Worldchanger #1

MIRANDA WAS ALWAYS COMPARING HERSELF WITH OTHERS, wishing she had nicer clothes, a sportier car, and an unlimited charge card. When she got to the University of Illinois, she turned her back on God to run with the fast crowd who were into seeking thrills and obtaining material possessions. She spent two years chasing this dream, trying to fill the emptiness in her soul, only to come to a dead end one day when, after receiving a notice that her $10,000 credit card limit had reached its max, she purposely got drunk and ran her convertible into a tree.

Now in intensive care, Miranda had plenty of time to reflect on her life and the choices she'd made. After being released, she went back to her apartment, got on her knees and returned to God to search for *real* meaning. A friend brought her to a Christian meeting, and it so happened the program that evening consisted of a visiting band of missions mobilizers called **The Traveling Team** who went from campus to campus each night sharing the story of God's heart for the nations.

Miranda sat mesmerized, learning God had given her all these different blessings in life (health, education, finances, technology, salvation, the Bible, etc...) not to horde for herself, but to give away. She realized she was a "taker" rather than a "giver" and became resolute about making a real difference in the world. She set up an appointment with one of The Traveling Team representatives to talk the next morning. As they chatted, Miranda started to see her whole life flash before her, and this confident, self-sufficient girl broke down crying, repenting of her selfishness and her "bless *me* Lord!" kind of inward-focused Christianity.

The Traveling Team rep plotted out a timeline for spiritual growth and mission involvement for Miranda and then connected her with a more mature believer on campus. Together, they started meeting for quiet times, Bible study, and praying for the spiritually lost around the world. A year later, Miranda finally got to go with a summer mission team to Ukraine, where she spent two months sharing the gospel. By the fifth week she was hooked. She no longer cared what others possessed and what she didn't, but instead became eternally grateful for *all* that God had blessed her with and purposed to spend her life giving it away to the desperate and separated from Christ.

She came back to campus that fall a changed woman, serving and sharing the Lord with every international student she could. Now, about to graduate and offered a high-paying position with a huge company, she instead wants to teach English in a closed third-world country. She has real, lasting fulfillment in her heart, finding the joy that only comes when we say no to ourselves and yes to God.

Worldchanger #2

Peter was a freshman involved with **InterVarsity Christian Fellowship** (IV) at the University of Wisconsin-Madison when he and some of his Christian buddies decided to get serious about reaching others for Christ. Rick Richardson, author of *Evangelism Outside the Box*, and IV staffer in Madison at the time, was diligently praying that Peter and other students would take personal ownership of the ministry there. God answered as Peter and six other freshmen began meeting every Tuesday at 5:30 p.m. to pray, confess their sins, and intercede for the campus. The Lord began to burden them for their lost friends, and Peter, without knowing any better, invited one of them to join the group for prayer. This wasn't just any non-believer, according to Richardson, he was a "cosmic-consciousness, pot-smoking, drug-and-alcohol-using student, who had sampled Marxist and New Age thinking, and decided to embrace atheism."

Although everyone was a little uncomfortable with the new addition to the group, they proceeded as usual with the worship, confession, and intercession. But as the meeting concluded, and the students began exiting, Daniel, the non-Christian friend that Peter had brought, raced over to confront him with a question.

"What was *that*?!" Daniel demanded.

"What was *what*?!" Peter responded nervously.

"I don't even *believe* in God, but *God* was in that room. What happened?"

After spending three hours explaining the gospel to Daniel, this outspoken atheist bowed in prayer to begin a personal relationship with Jesus.

What convinced this hardened scoffer? Daniel had encountered the presence of God in an authentic, Spirit-filled community and would never be the same. When the story of his radical conversion got back to the other six freshmen in the prayer group, they all immediately began inviting *their* non-Christian friends to the meetings! Over 25 students found the Savior that year through the IV freshman prayer gathering. Peter and his friends were determined to seek God's face until He showed up in very tangible ways. And show up He did!

Worldchanger #3

Jennifer grew up in a neat Christian family in South Georgia, but as she began her freshman year at West Georgia College, she asked God to give her someone who could help her understand her mission and calling in Christ. The ministry of **Campus Outreach** (CO) was engaging in their own version of "Christian Rush," (recruiting freshmen to get involved with their ministry), and Jennifer happened to meet up with Lisa, a CO staff member. As they got to know each other, Jennifer was drawn to Lisa's fun, personal way of talking with her and freely sharing her faith with others. Jennifer's spiritual hunger and faithfulness was very evident, so Lisa began to pour into her on a regular basis. They would study the Word together, go on evangelism and follow-up appointments, do contact work in the dorms, and start small groups among interested girls.

Jennifer was a woman of application, and everything that Lisa told her and showed her, she sought to implement into her own personal ministry. By Jennifer's senior year, she'd seen over twenty women come to Christ, had several discipleship groups going, and met one on one with a number of girls. She got so excited about equipping her disciples to begin ministering, she decided she wanted to do it full time. Now Jennifer is a CO staff member too, at Georgia College, where the last few years, hundreds of women have come to Christ through her witness and the student leaders she's equipped. Last year, 121 female students from their campus attended their annual Christmas Conference and 50 of those came to their summer-long training program. She is leaving behind a wake of impact that will last clear into eternity.

Worldchanger #4

Tony grew up in Taiwan before coming to America to attend college. Although he had gone to church as a boy, he purposed *not* to listen and deemed it "a waste of a Sunday morning." Now, at the University of Oklahoma, he was far away from family, and he began drinking excessively with older students. Although he felt miserable, he continued, and his habit became addictive. Late one night, his hands started shaking uncontrollably. Desperately looking for some alcohol to calm his nerves, the phone rang, and it was a Christian guy he'd met who was involved there in the **Baptist Collegiate Ministry** (BCM). The Lord used that phone call to get his attention, and that evening he finally admitted that God was all-powerful and all-loving and wanted to forgive Tony if only he would confess his sin and repent. Ending his session with the Lord, he prayed, "Please change me. Help me to live according to the Bible."

Tony determined to leave behind his drinking and worldly lifestyle. Aaron, the leader of a BCM floor Bible study started meeting with Tony each week, working on Scripture memory, quiet times, and Christ-like living. They would go out witnessing together and Tony realized how inward and selfish he'd been and committed to the Lord to share the gospel with one student each day. Tony says he prays for daily opportunities and sometimes "God gives me two or three to witness to instead of just one!"

Like Aaron had done, Tony searched and found a dorm floor where no other committed Christian lived. His prayer goal is to reach out to every student on the floor, declaring that his semester began "the day the freshmen moved in." Along with his relationship building and witnessing, he has started a small group Bible study on his floor and has already begun discipling Cole and Tyler. This sophomore from Taiwan wants to be a soldier for Jesus Christ and has adopted as his marching orders the Great Commission found in Matthew 28:18-20 to "make disciples of all nations..."

Worldchanger #5

Jordan grew up camping, hiking, and rock climbing with full intentions of passionately pursuing these loves when he entered the University of Arkansas—but God had a different plan. A **Campus Crusade for Christ** (CCC) staff member plugged him into a small group and their leadership training track. Jordan went to a CCC Summer Project in Missouri and one in the country of Estonia the next summer. He was so jazzed by how God used him, he changed his major to graduate sooner, raised support, and headed to Thailand for a year-long mission assignment.

Jordan is an adventurer, and when he first got to Thailand, he traveled with a team showing the *Jesus Film* to eager tribes of natives who had never even seen a movie. One night, as the entire tribe's eyes were locked on the screen, God touched many of their hearts. Jordan was impacted too, sharing, "The Lord really spoke to me that night. My dreams were coming true: being out in the wilderness and showing the *Jesus Film* to those who have never heard. Just to look at the people's eyes during the film was amazing. It was one of the greatest nights of my life."

His main ministry, though, is to the one million college students in the bustling, pollution-filled city of Bangkok. After overcoming culture shock from the abject poverty, the putrid smell, even the swarms of stray dogs everywhere, he was able to settle down and build relationships with Thai students. Jordan is sharing the gospel on a daily basis, seeing some receive Christ and others rejecting Him because of their Buddhist beliefs. He agonizes over the hardened hearts and, when one guy responded to his gospel message with, "I don't need Jesus," Jordan just about broke down and cried. It's hard to believe that this happy-go-lucky kid from Harrison, Arkansas, who had his life all planned out is now, instead, half way across the world pouring his life out for the lost in Thailand.

The Box:
Make a list of students you know on your campus who need to be witnessed to or discipled. Will you take the lead?

Seven Secrets to Avoid Persecution
Part One

SEVEN. THE PERFECT NUMBER. SURELY ANY LIST OF SEVEN *must* be divinely inspired. You might want to get into the lotus position to slowly absorb this heavenly information into your cranial lobes. Allow it to trickle down into your heart and see if it doesn't give you a whole bunch of warm fuzzys inside. You might even get to experience the ultimate verification as to whether or not this list is from God: goose bumps!

The topic, though, works against me: Persecution. We Christians run from the "P word" faster than we do the "E word" (Evangelism) or the "M word" (Missions). And, of course, persecution starts with "p" and so does the word "pain." I confess, over the years, I have spent more time watching movies than I have studying my Bible, and as a result, when I hear a word (like "pain") I instantly think of a movie clip rather than a Scripture verse.

During the classic movie *ROCKY 3*, a sports writer asked the huge, muscle-bound, gold-laden, mohawk-wearing Clubber Lang what his prediction was before his big title fight with the older and smaller Rocky Balboa.

"Prediction?" he gruffly repeated the question back at the intimidated reporter.

"Pain!" was Clubber's sinister one word response, forecasting the beating he was about to give the champ.

Me? I avoid pain at all costs. I run from it. I surround my life with as many comforts, conveniences, securities and insurances I possibly can. If pain or persecution even hints at coming my way, I instantly and desperately find a way to slither out and escape. The Christian life is supposed to be easy, soft, smooth—that's a sign you've *really* been blessed by God. Right? When problems, pain, and persecution come your way, it must be God punishing you. But then my theological bubble bursts when I read a verse like 2 Timothy 3:12 where Paul says,

> "Indeed, all who desire to live godly in Christ Jesus WILL BE persecuted." (emphasis mine)

How can this be? You're trying to tell me that if I'm not experiencing any persecution,* it may be because I'm not seeking to live a godly life in Christ? I resent that! I know that verse *sounds* like a promise, but surely we could find some "scholar" somewhere to vouch for us that this passage was miscopied by a farsighted 3rd century scribe. If not, I'm going to pronounce *myself* a "scholar" and begin my own website:

www.LoopHolesforChrist.com.

Besides, who is *truly* able to objectively distinguish fact from fiction in this antiquated book we call The Bible?

I'm like one of the self-revered, 1st century Gnostics—holy men who possessed a "secret knowledge" that gave them salvation and the inside track to God and His ways. You too can experience superior intelligence and existential vibrations if you will only join my exclusive "Gnostic Junior" club and follow these seven simple, but profound secrets. But don't write them down anywhere. Just memorize and utilize:

*Did you know that while we are praying that the underground church believers in China won't experience persecution, they are praying that we American Christians will?! Do they know something we don't?

Secret #1: Choose tolerance over truth

My philosophy teacher says the key to worldwide unity is diversity and multiculturalism. Appreciating and giving *equal* value to any and all beliefs is the sign of genuine maturity and love. Chill out...who can *really* know what is true anyway? My antenna says this guy must know what he's talking about. He's got a Ph.D., a 30-year tenured professorship, and a long beard. Talk about credibility!

I confess. I want everybody to like me. I came *so* close to winning the "Most Popular" award my senior year in High School. My strategy was to smile at everyone, call them by name, act like I was really interested in what they were saying, and agree with *any* point they made. Regardless of what wild, immoral, or perverse heresy they came up with, my standard answer was, "Yeah, that's awesome!" A few of my friends say I'm easily swayed and that they saw *my* picture right next to the definition of the word "gullible" in the dictionary!

I haven't looked it up yet.

I know that the Voice of the Martyrs ministry and the DC Talk band wrote some leathery looking book a while back called *Jesus Freaks* that describes different men and women who stood up for truth and it cost them their lives. But that stuff is about *other* people in *other* lands in *other* times. It's old, outdated and definitely not for me. Some boring kids at school claim to know "the truth" and are taking heat for it. Me, I'm staying cool and choosing tolerance.

Secret #2: Don't *ever* say there's only one way to God

I tried this once. Never again! I had been witnessing to students at a liberal, liberal arts college with a denominational affiliation. Explaining the gospel is one thing, but I foolishly made the mistake of asking different students to receive Jesus Christ into their lives after assuring them that it was the only way to obtain eternal forgiveness. The two chaplains at this small college caught wind of it and called me into their office. Boy, were their neck veins bulging and faces red. After slamming the door and sitting down across from me, they pointed their finger at me and yelled, "You're nothing but a religious exclusionist!"

"That doesn't sound too complimentary" I said, "What do you mean?"

"You believe there's only *one* way to God!" they shot back.

"Well," I started, "John 14:6 says, 'I am the way, the truth, and the life, no one comes to the Father but through Me.'"

"That's *your* interpretation!" they angrily shouted.

"My interpretation?" I protested, "Jesus is the one who said it, not me!"

As you can imagine, I felt attacked, maligned, and absolutely archaic in my narrow little doctrines. I vowed never to get in that situation again and concluded God is certainly big enough to create many paths up the mountain. Sincerity is the key, not slavery to some tightly restricted "magic formula." I wisely rethought my "only one way" philosophy in order to fit in better with the culture.

Secret #3: Never ask anyone the "golden question"

After presenting the gospel to someone, the "golden question" is the most agonizingly difficult string of words in the human language to utter. Even typing it out, my hands are sweating, my heart is pounding, and my throat is dry. Here goes:

> *"Zack, I was, uh, wondering if you, um, would want to, uh, consider…the possibility of, um, maybe thinking about, well… inviting Christ, uh, into your life…as, ya' know, your Lord and, um, your Savior…maybe even (cough, cough) right now?"*

Posing that question to someone, locking my eyes onto theirs, and then zipping up my lip to wait for their response is harder to do than swallowing rancid pig intestines on a reality TV show. But, at no time in that person's life will the Holy Spirit have more of an opportunity to bring "divine pressure" on them than those few awkward seconds of silence after they've been asked the "golden question!"

The problem is they might say "no" and I *hate* to be rejected. Who likes to make people feel uncomfortable anyway? Why play Sherlock Holmes with my offensive interrogations when God can surely save them without the aid of my scrawny little questions?

Secret #4: Assume all people are Christians and going to heaven

I know Jesus said that most people are headed down the broad road to destruction and very few down the narrow path to salvation. But what about purgatory? I know it's not in the Bible, but it makes so much sense. Besides, wouldn't it be just like God to, in the end, forgive *everyone*? It would really prove, once and for all, His ultimate kindness and mercy. Come on now. Say it slowly with me: "Wouldn't it be just like God to forgive *everyone*?"

Some mission experts tell us that about 23 people die every ten seconds, and 19 of them pass into a Christ*less* eternity. Riiiight! Where in the world did they get that figure? I think I put more stock in my teenage son's claim: "Dad, did you know that 95% of all statistics are made up on the spot?" Polls have shown most all Americans believe in God, have gone to church, own a Bible, and even put a dollar or two in the red Salvation Army bucket at Christmas time. They certainly look like Christians to me. Furthermore, when I ask them if they are, they say they are. Isn't that good enough?

The Box:
Think back and try to remember the times you have had any kind of persecution for your faith (rejection, ridicule, anything?).

Now quick, turn the page! The knee-deep sarcasm continues in Part Two!

Seven Secrets to Avoid Persecution
Part Two

Secret #5: Don't make any enemies

Did Jesus *really* say "Do not think that I came to bring peace on the earth; I did not come to bring peace, but a sword" in Matthew 10:34? If so, Jesus really pours fuel on the fire by then saying He wants to set a son against his father, daughter against her mother, etc....Did He truly intend for the gospel to drive a wedge into families? I thought He wanted to unite families, not separate them! I can't believe my kind, sweet, polite Jesus wants people divided. *My* bumper sticker says: *Pray for World Peace.* How about yours?

I know they've doctored up history some when they tell of the incredible faith and courage the 1st century Christians demonstrated as they were ripped apart by the famished wild animals being cheered on by the bloodthirsty coliseum crowd. The Romans were used to seeing the victims screaming, cursing, and kicking as they were dragged in. The Christians, though, would actually *volunteer* and *line up* to get the chance to die for Christ. Then they would walk calmly to the center of the arena singing hymns to God, passively allowing themselves to be totally ravished. No wonder the raucous mob would grow silent, and out of respect and total amazement, turn to each other and whisper,

"See how these Christians die!" The Roman emperors were befuddled too as they pondered, "How do you destroy a faith, a movement, a person…who is not afraid to die?"

And as it relates to sharing the gospel, I have a checkered past, with a record of making huge mistakes, producing some very painful scars I certainly don't want to dredge up or ever allow happen again. Like the time a member of my fraternity exploded into my room early one morning while I was still asleep, rushed over to my bed, put his beer-breathed face right up against mine, screaming "if you ever cram your religion down one more pledge's throat, I will knock the #*@%>*, ^"(*@#%* out of you!"

"Well, good morning to you too!" I thought.

I know 1 Peter 4:14 says "If you are reviled for the name of Christ, you are blessed." If *that's* a blessing, all I have to say is "Thanks, but no thanks!"

Secret #6: Let your *life* just be your witness, *not* your words

OK, OK, I know Jesus spoke out and was put to death. But He was the Son of God. I know Paul and Peter and Stephen spoke out and it cost them their lives too. But they were special. I can't compare myself to them. They were like, *really* filled with the Holy Spirit, and it sure seems back then the Holy Spirit was a lot more powerful than He is now.

When I lived in the fraternity house I would stand up at dinner each week and announce the time and location of that night's "College Life" campus ministry meeting. Immediately, a group of snickering guys at the other end of the dining hall would blatantly mock me by announcing to everyone when that night's "Wild Life" meeting would be held at the local bar. I still wake up in the middle of the night in a cold sweat remembering the way they would laugh at me. Never again!

I understand Revelation 12:11 says the apostles overcame Satan because of "the blood of the Lamb and because of the *word* of their testimony" and that they "did not love their life even faced with death." But we can be smarter than they were by knowing when to keep our mouth shut. I call it "safe witnessing", where I apply my poker philosophy of "you gotta know when to hold 'em and know when to fold 'em."

Anyway, you don't need to actually *share* the gospel to make impact. I prefer to just "let my light shine." A smile on my face, a fish on my car, and a verse on my T-shirt will let them know the way to God. Right on?

Secret #7: Don't even *think* about missions

Hey, it's a cold, dark, violent world out there. The nightly news anchors tell us that everyone hates Americans and resents our attitudes, lifestyles and religion. Your mom and dad are right when they say, "You shouldn't spend the summer in China or Africa, it's too dangerous. What if you're kidnapped? What if you get sick? What if the authorities find out you're a missionary?"

Stay here this summer. Find a job. Make some money. Get a suntan. Have some fun. Hang out with your friends. Go to the beach. Be a college student. Enjoy it while it lasts. There'll be plenty of time for mission trips later in life. Don't make waves. You have *so* much going for you, why risk your future?

And if you do go, *please* don't witness. You're just there just to build houses, teach English and be a "do gooder" American. Besides, it might be against the law. I know the apostle Peter told the authorities "we must obey God rather than men" in response to their ultimatum for him to quit preaching. But me, I'm into keeping the laws, and furthermore, isn't a good Christian a good citizen too?

You see, I am on a one man crusade to stomp out *any* persecution in this country. I have my rights you know! If *anyone* dares to discriminate against me or oppose me, I'm going to bring a lawsuit against them. I know the Bible says something about 'if they slap you on one cheek turn the other, or if they steal your coat, give them your shirt too,' but my role model is Popeye the Sailor Man, who says, "Tha's all I can stands, and I can't stands no more!"

But some say we should *welcome* persecution. Can you believe that? Some radicals even think we should *pray* for it. No way! Some right wing fundamentalists claim history shows the Church grows and thrives under persecution and becomes weak and ineffective when there is no opposition. I don't care. I'm living for the here and now, and I believe God is committed to blessing *our* country, protecting *our* country, keeping *us* out of harm's way. Persecution? That's surely for other less fortunate, less blessed, less wise countries than us. We are, after all, a great and godly Christian nation.

Aren't we?

For me, though, it's out of sight, out of mind. The www.Persecution.com people claim 165,000 people are martyred each year for their Christian faith somewhere around the world. That's hard to believe, isn't it? I mean, no one on my campus has been killed this year because of their Christian faith. How 'bout on yours?

There's no need for anyone to get worked up or fanatical about all this. Take it easy. Go play a video game. Go buy a romance novel. Go watch a sitcom or maybe plug in one of your favorite praise CD's. Get your mind off of pain or persecution.

The "P" word—don't even think about it.

In fact, don't worry—be happy.

The Box:
If 2 Timothy 3:12 (All who desire godly in Christ Jesus will be persecuted) is true, then what are some things you can do to insure you will be persecuted for Christ's sake?

Leaving a Legacy
Sospeso

In the cafés of Naples, Italy some kind hearted patrons order a Sospeso or coffee "in suspense." When doing this you pay for two coffees, one for yourself and the other for a needy future customer who walks in off the street to ask if there are any coffees held in suspense.

We have a choice in life. We can live for ourselves or we can live for others. Selfishness or selflessness. Why not decide today to leave an eternal legacy by influencing others for Jesus Christ?

Three Secrets from the Buzz Underwood Files: Shock Therapy Discipleship

I HAD TWO DIFFERENT MEN DISCIPLE ME IN COLLEGE. THE first took me through ministry materials each week, along with the "mandatory" one-on-one we had agreed on. At the end of my freshman year, he graduated, we shook hands, and I've never heard from him since! That experience taught me that discipleship involves giving a young believer some direction, yes, but requires the pouring out of some affection too. Later in college, God gave me a second man, Buzz (that's right, Buzz) Underwood, as my discipler who loved me in spite of myself. I'd never met someone who cared, served, prayed and invested in my life like Buzz did. He didn't do it to impress others or even out of obedience to God; he did it because he enjoyed being with me, the highest compliment you can pay anyone.

Buzz was the Apostle Paul at my college, and if you were going to hang with him, you would instantly be labeled a Christian extremist and inevitably be ostracized by certain campus factions. Like a modern day Dr. Jekyl and Mr. Hyde, part of me still wanted to be cool and accepted by my fraternity brothers and at the same time appear spiritually radical to the other Christians on campus. Buzz helped me change all that with his version of shock therapy discipleship taken from Paul's second letter to Timothy, his young disciple. Even though my safe, comfortable life was traumatized, I forever learned three of Buzz's paradigm-shifting secrets of turning Christians into disciples.

Secret #1: Expose the embarrassment

Buzz was a senior ROTC (Reserves Officer Training Corps) student who doubled as a Resident Assistant in a men's dorm, but from all appearances his primary goal in life was to show *me* how ashamed I was of the gospel! One night as I was coming over to his dorm for our weekly small group, Buzz happened to hop on the elevator at the last second. Instead of greeting me, he casually leaned up against the side of the crowded elevator and acting like he didn't know me, said, "Hey buddy. What's that in your hand?" Of course, all 12 sets of eyes were glued to the flashing floor numbers above, pretending they weren't listening to *every single word* exchanged between Buzz and me.

Pausing to catch my breath, I sheepishly responded in a low voice, "It's a Bible, Buzz."

"*A Bible!*" he shouted, "That's not that stuff that talks about Jesus Christ being the *Son of God*, is it?!"

After turning eighteen shades of red, I finally lowered my head and whispered, "Yeah, Buzz. That's what it says."

He wasn't through with his thrashing, though, and added, "You don't really *believe* that stuff, do you?"

Luckily, the door to our floor opened, and I was rescued from having to answer his final question.

Even though I wanted to vanish from the face of the earth during those painfully drawn out seconds on the elevator, I later was very grateful to Buzz, who exposed my unwillingness to *totally* identify with Jesus Christ, the Scriptures and, Buzz himself. As cruel as it seems, he was only trying to help me, even as the Apostle Paul challenged young

Timothy:

> "Do not be ashamed to testify about our Lord, or be ashamed of me His prisoner, but join with me in suffering for the gospel, by the power of God." (2 Timothy 1:8)

Little did I know that my training had just begun…

Secret #2: Prepare for impact

A few weeks later Buzz asked me to go with him to visit a Resident Assistant friend of his in a nearby dorm. I agreed, not fully comprehending yet that Buzz was into teaching me "object lessons" wherever we went! So up we zoomed to the 10th story, but when the elevator door opened, we couldn't get out because of the 60 freshmen packed in together, waiting for a floor meeting to begin. As we squeezed out from the closing elevator, I looked around at the sea of guys sitting and staring up at us. Instantly, Buzz's friend recognized us and said, "Buzz, good to have you with us tonight. I'll turn it over to you." Without hesitation, Buzz, imitating a late night talk show host, warmed up the crowd by announcing, "It's great to be with you guys. I want to introduce our speaker tonight." He then turns to me, and through his devious smile simply says… "You're on." Shocked and absolutely appalled, I rotated my head from Buzz's grin to the waiting eyes of my young audience. "Well….um, it is, uh, good to be with, uh, you guys tonight", nervously studdering and stalling all the way.

I really don't recall details of what I said over the next fifteen minutes or so, but I do remember gaining enough composure to move into my personal testimony and then into a gospel explanation. Later, it was obvious to me that this was a total set up and that Buzz was trying to "prime the pump" by putting me in a situation to see if I would be willing and able to share my faith, without *even* a moment's notice! Again, I see a parallel in how hesitant and timid Timothy was, but still Paul exhorted him in 2 Timothy 4:2 to "preach the Word; be ready in season and out of season…" I was starting to see this Great Commission thing was 24 hours a day, seven days a week, and Buzz was preparing me to impact others for Christ anywhere, anytime. He knew, though, that the outer witness was only as strong as the inward character, and although I pretended to be modest, I still had an ego the size of Texas…

Secret # 3: Love the unlovable

You see, I *thought* I was the campus Billy Graham until I met Buzz, and even though I was like a wild bucking bronco when it came to respecting or submitting to his spiritual leadership, he never gave up on me. Buzz and I lived together my senior year, where he would constantly make my bed and fix the meals. I repaid his kindnesses by begrudgingly sitting in his early morning bible study with a blanket wrapped around my head to protest the ungodly hour!

Once, during a prayer walk we took together, in the middle of his very sincere petition, I glared at his bowed head and scoffed, "You're the biggest phony I've *ever* met!" If there was ever a time I deserved for someone to call me a slimy imbecile and whack me, it was then. Instead, he patiently smiled, put his hand on my shoulder, looked right into my eyes, and soul, then quietly uttered four unbelievable words, "I love you bro." That was the final straw! All of my defenses totally broke down and my rebellious heart melted into surrender as I finally grasped how authentic his love was for me. Like Jesus, instead of striking back, he absorbed my assault and extended kindness in return. In 2 Timothy 4:24, 25 Paul instructed Timothy to do likewise: "The Lord's bondservant must not be quarrelsome, but be kind to all, able to teach, patient when wrong, with gentleness correcting those who are in opposition." I realized that I had been against leadership unless, of course, I was the leader! The real phony was staring back at me in the mirror as I tried to hide my arrogance with a humility performance that could have won me an Oscar!

Finally broken, I remember the exact day and place I was walking in front of the school library where I made the *once and for all* decision that I would be one person, not two! I'd been playing both sides of the fence, but with Buzz's help, was determined not to allow other's opinions to paralyze me any longer. From that point on, I was going to walk toward my fears, forsaking my "esteemed reputation" in favor of suffering for the gospel, like Paul modeled to Timothy. Renouncing *my* agenda to fulfill God's, I yearned for Him to light the flame of revival on my campus, but ultimately understood that He wanted to use my life as the fuel. Buzz's version of shock therapy discipleship had dramatically impacted me. Sometimes moving from simply a "run of the mill" Christian to a radical disciple requires drastic measures!

Thanks Buzz!

The Box:
Are there any areas of vision or skills you can grow in? Name a person or two who might be willing to help (i.e. disciple) you in these areas.

One Spiritual Arsonist
I Want You to Meet

MATT WAS THE LAST ONE TO STAND UP. HE HAD BEEN waiting for this day an entire year. Finally the night arrived where he and five other graduating seniors in their fraternity would give a farewell speech to all 80 of their Greek brothers. Even though most of their chapter meetings were full of drinking and laughing, the custom for this one was different. All eyes and ears were glued to the six men who were allowed to talk as long as they wanted (and say anything they wanted) to the underclassmen who were listening with rapt attention.

Sadly, all six men squandered this opportunity of a lifetime, except one: Matt. The first five only took two or three minutes to empty their brain by spitting out such insightful statements as: "it's been fun" and "keep your selves out of trouble." No one had really expected much depth, though, from guys who had shown them selves to be so shallow over the years.

It was different for Matt. He had loved and served these men for four years, doing the dirty work no one else was willing to do. Everyone knew he was the hardest working leader on campus and had often been recruited to run for Student Body President and Fraternity President. Matt would turn them down each time. The reason? He wanted to use all of his free time to *individually* share the gospel with each member and pledge in his chapter. I know he did. I was with him at least ten of those appointments where he would draw out the gospel, answer questions, and then look deep into the eyes of his young friend and ask, "Would you like to invite Jesus Christ into your life as *your* Lord and Savior?" Gently asking that question, and then patiently waiting for an answer was Matt's passion and calling from God.

You see, Matt is what I call a "Spiritual Arsonist." No, he isn't a religious fanatic trying to torch the administrative buildings in the middle of the night. Instead, Matt's goal is to ignite a holy fire that would burn bright in his fraternity and spread to the entire university.

> In short, he wanted to turn his college upside down
> for the Lord Jesus Christ.

He chose to strike his match at the most explosive place of all—the top fraternity on campus. The risks were high, but the potential results were huge.

Well, back to the meeting. Matt started by re-explaining the gospel message to all the guys and then asking them to raise their hand if they had made that decision and considered themselves a Christian. Almost all eighty guys raised their hand. "I was afraid of that!" Matt sighed. He knows that most students, especially in the South, have grown up *thinking* they are Christians because they're Americans, own a Bible, have a mother, or can spell c-h-u-r-c-h.

Matt then turned to Matthew 7:20-21 and read:

> "So then, you will know them by their fruits. Not everyone who says to Me, 'Lord, Lord' will enter the kingdom of heaven, but he who does the will of My Father who is in heaven will enter."

After sharing his own personal testimony and the changes Christ made in his life, Matt went on to read and explain Matthew 7:22-23:

> *"Many will say to Me on that day, 'Lord, Lord, did we not prophesy in Your name, and in Your name cast out demons, and in Your name perform many miracles?' And then I will declare to them, 'I never knew you; depart from Me, you who practice lawlessness.'"*

Then Matt walked to the middle of the room and looked around. He solemnly said, "Now that you know that a real Christian is someone who is a sold out follower of Jesus Christ who only does the will of the Father, I'd like to ask you again,

> *"If anyone would like to publicly acknowledge Jesus Christ as the Lord and Savior of your life…*
>
> *…stand up right now."*

No one dared move. No one even breathed. Every single eye was riveted on Matt. He calmly scanned the room, one by one returning each person's gaze, and waiting for the first man to make his move. What seemed like eternity was really only about 180 seconds of death—still—quiet.

Finally, one guy stood up with his head bowed. A second popped up and then a third. That was all. Even though it was only three out of 80, inwardly Matt was relieved. These three were the only ones in the entire group who *really* were Christians. Matt was proud of them for openly identifying with Christ. At least everyone in the room now knew the difference between the "professors" and the "possessors" of the Christian faith.

But Matt was now faced with a decision himself. What was he going to say to the remaining 77 men who chose not to stand up to "prove" their commitment to Christ? He loved them and desperately wanted them to turn from their sin and follow the one true God.

He decided to give the group a short history lesson from the Old Testament and explained the cycle the Israelites went through over and over again:

1. They would repent and follow God
2. God would then bless them abundantly
3. They would then forget about God and worship idols instead
4. God would need to punish them to get their attention
5. Israel would once again repent and follow God

So Matt then showed his fraternity brothers how this sequence of "repentance and reconciliation" applied to them and why they should take the holiness of God seriously:

> *God is a righteous judge, and a God who has indignation every day. If a man does not repent, He will sharpen His sword; He has bent His bow and made it ready."* (Psalm 7:11,12)

With head bent and heart heavy, Matt tenderly stated,

> *"Men, I did not want to do this. I love each of you guys and want the very best for you. But, because I care for you so much, I am going to pray for your destruction. I am going to pray for the fraternity's destruction and each of your individual destruction until you are willing to repent and humble yourselves before God."*

With stunned and confused looks on the faces of all 80 men, Matt lowered his head and specifically prayed for the destruction of the entire fraternity (as well as each individual member) until they turned from their sin and gave their hearts to Jesus Christ.

Finishing his prayer, Matt looked up to see several of the guys looking at their cell phones. It turns out that at the exact time Matt was praying for their destruction, many of the members were receiving text messages sent to them by a rival fraternity (made up of a number of large football players) who were on their way over at that very moment to beat them up for a past offense. As each man finished reading the text message on his screen, he looked up at Matt with wide open eyes and gaping mouth.

The air in that room was now so thick with the overpowering presence and fury of God, it was almost suffocating. Everyone knew this was no coincidence. The chapter's graduate advisor, who had been the biggest partier on the campus, stood up and said, "Matt, this is from God. What should we do?"

Matt has been answering that question and many others from the men in that chapter room in the days since "the meeting." No, the rival fraternity never followed through on their threats, but the fear of God has been implanted in the hearts of Matt's so-called "brothers." During their lifetime, they will forget the contents of a thousand different meetings, but each of those men are sure to remember every single word spoken by Matt on Senior Night, April 20, 2004. And no, I am not necessarily recommending you pray for the destruction of the non-believers around you. God is plenty able to bring divine pressure on his creatures without your help or mine!

But a question remains: What would possess a friendly and gifted college student like Matt to give up the accolades of being the BMOC (Big Man on Campus) in exchange for the fear and loathing he received from others?

> He could have had all the titles, all the girls, all the popularity
> he wanted, but instead, blazed a path of a different kind.

This graduating senior was consumed with the glory of God on earth. His desire was to spend every waking moment pointing others to the Savior, multiplying white hot worshippers across the planet.

Matt may not remember the old campfire song "It only takes a spark to get a fire going," but then again, he didn't need to. He was living it out—one person at a time, one fraternity at a time, one campus at a time, one nation at a time. You see, a true member of the "Arsonists for Christ" club seeks to ignite a fire of eternal consequence *wherever* God leads them. Their location or vocation is not near as important as living a life of reckless abandonment to the person and purposes of Jesus Christ.

How about you?
Why are you at college?

What club(s) are you part of? Does the "Light of the World" live inside your heart? Don't hide Jesus under a basket. Let Him out. Your campus desperately needs Him—and you. It only takes a spark. Be that spark. Go ahead…light it up!

Epilogue: You might be wondering what Matt is up to now that he is an official graduate. He just got back from spending a year in Hyderabad, India reaching out to high caste Hindu college students. Recently, he finished raising his personal financial support team and is back at his alma mater as a full time campus minister. I happen to ask him which groups on campus he is targeting with his evangelistic and discipling efforts. Of course, his old fraternity is at the top of his list! In fact, he has already taken *every* single pledge through the gospel and asked each one the golden question: "Would you like to invite Jesus Christ into *your* life as your Lord and Savior—right now?" Oh yeah. It only takes a spark to get a fire going!

The Box:
What groups (living group, social club, intramural team, etc…) are you part of on your campus? How could God use *you* to ignite a fire for Christ in them?

Four Extraordinary Flashmobs

Wild and rambunctious hordes of uncontrolled enthusiasm.
Sound like fun?

Outrageous and riotous crowds of untamed lunacy.
Wanna' join in?

No, WE ARE NOT TALKING ABOUT THE PROTESTS OF THE 60'S or even the streaking* of the 70's. We are referring to the more recent phenomena among college students (and other slightly eccentric "adults") who simultaneously converge on unsuspecting locations to perform—as a group—a pre-planned, but totally illogical, act. Yes, they all meet somewhere together—even though they are all *absolute* strangers.

It's called a "flashmob" and has become popular the last several years among the internet generation, who receive their recreational marching orders from the little box on their desk connected to the world. They log on to sites like www.FlashMob.com to find out where and when the next harebrained "performance" was scheduled in their city or campus.

*Large groups of college students (mainly guys, but some girls mixed in!) would congregate late at night in a specific agreed on place. They would then take off all their clothes (except maybe a ski mask) and run stark naked right through the middle of campus, sometimes with hundreds (thousands?) of other students cheering them on.

For example:

In Cambridge, Massachusetts, nearly 200 people descended upon the Harvard bookstore, mobbing the store's greeting card section, all looking for a card for a friend named Bill.

In Denver, Colorado, a large group appeared for ten minutes at a mall, counted backwards from 60 to zero, mimicked playing ping pong against the floor—and then they were gone.

In Sao Paolo, Brazil 100 people showed up in the middle of the city's main avenue, took off one of their shoes, repeatedly banged it on the street, and disappeared.

I counted 75 postings listing flashmobs all over the U.S. and in other countries. From Seattle to Jacksonville, from London to Hong Kong, everyone wanted to get in on these temporary moments of insanity.

We dare not print post #75, though, recorded at 12:12 a.m. last night, lest we quench all this youthful hysteria. Okay, here it is anyway:

 "What is the point of this......are you all social degenerates? Get a life and do something more worthwhile than this! How incredibly sad. "

Robert Zazueta, founder of www.FlockSmart.com, another organizer of flashmobs, counters disparaging post #75: "Some people see it as performance art, others a social outlet. Still others just see it as a way to freak out the tourists!"

The more I think about it, the more I believe flashmobs are not anything new. In fact, one of my favorite reads—the Bible—records a number of unruly, "out of control" human convergences that literally changed the world. This best-seller of all time gives us incredible insights into the human psyche by describing *God's version* of four flashmobs that He used to turn the world "right side up." Let me describe them:

Flashmob #1 at Shinar—Genesis 11

After the flood, God once again commanded the people to spread out, be fruitful, and multiply. Instead, they all chose to assemble at the plain of Shinar (modern day Iraq) and build a tower reaching up into heaven. Their goal was to combine their common language and strengths to oppose the plan of God and to "make a name for ourselves."

If they were not going to voluntarily obey the Lord's decree, then He would need to take action against this flashmob of a crowd. It was here that God gave every family a different language, and thus forced them to "scatter abroad over the face of the earth." The Lord of creation wanted the *whole* earth to be filled with His glory, not just Shinar…

Flashmob #2 in the Upper Room—Luke 24

Jesus had been brutally killed—unjustly nailed to a Roman cross. Now His disciples were on the run, hiding from the authorities, afraid they might face the same fate their Master had. Like desperate criminals, they rendezvoused at a secret location, making sure the door was dead bolted. Suddenly, the feeble, traumatized disciples froze, paralyzed with fear. Before their very eyes stood Jesus himself telling them "See My hands and My feet, that it is I Myself. Touch Me and see…"

At that moment, Christ opened their minds to understand the Scriptures, challenging them to leave their holy huddle and to proclaim repentance and forgiveness in His name "to all the nations." This late night encounter with the resurrected Christ instantly transformed this pitiful little flashmob into a growing band of radical revolutionaries—now ready to risk life and limb to take the gospel to the ends of the earth.

Flashmob #3 at the Jerusalem Gate—Acts 6-8

Right before He ascended, Jesus delivered His last sermon to His followers, commanding them to be His witnesses in Jerusalem, Judea, Samaria, and "even to the remotest part of the earth" (Acts 1:8). But Jerusalem was their city of choice, full of other believers and the comforts of life. And so…they stayed put. But the expansion and excitement of the newfound church encountered a major speed bump when the Sanhendrin (the Jewish religious council) decided to call in Stephen, an unsuspecting Christian leader, who was about to receive the grilling of a lifetime.

Responding to his interrogators, Stephen boldly proclaimed the gospel, finally pointing the finger at the Jewish leaders as the ones who murdered Jesus. They all "cried out with a loud voice, covered their ears and rushed at him with one impulse." Talk about a perfect description of a flashmob! The Sanhedrin and their followers then drug Stephen out of the city, and there, by the gate, stoned him to death. When word got around what had happened, a "great persecution against the church" broke out. The believers' safe and sound bubble of protection had burst and they were finally forced to do what Jesus had told them all along—to scatter throughout the regions to share the good news of salvation.

Flashmob #4 around the Throne—Revelation 7

The first three episodes I've described are history and can only be re-enacted in our own mind. But this fourth one is yet to come and, if we choose to, we can actually experience it. I'm telling you—you do not want to miss this one! This is the mother of all flashmobs and a "by invitation only" gathering that God Himself pulls together. It begins with the aged apostle John who's been exiled to the island of Patmos. First, God causes a deep sleep to come over him, and then proceeds to invade his mind with a series of mind-blowing visions describing how the Lord is going to culminate all of history.

We pick up the scene in heaven where all of God's angels, elders, and living creatures are falling on their faces in worship of Jesus Christ, the Lamb, seated on His throne. But John also sees a huge assembly of people packed in like sardines around this illuminated throne, with the glory and radiance of God Almighty emanating from it. With white robes on and waving palm branches, John described this throng as "a great multitude which no one could count, from every nation and all tribes and peoples and tongues…"

With every imaginable skin color there, what a gorgeous tapestry of human diversity God has woven! With every language on the planet represented, what a beautiful symphony of praise God has mixed together in perfect harmony! If you're a white, middle-class, Protestant American, you will no longer know what it means to be in the majority.

No, *if* you are there at the throne, you'll be surrounded by black skinned Africans jumping up and down, shouting their praise chants to God. Across the way you'll spot millions of Asian believers bowing low in quiet and humble adoration of their Savior. Glancing left and right, you'll be overwhelmed by the variety of dress, of customs, and of worship styles.

This flashmob, though, is not just a 10-minute interlude of mindless frivolity. No, around this throne, time and eternity stand still as every believer that has ever lived is now in the very presence of the King of Kings and Lord of Lords. A word of advice:

> You'll be spending all of eternity worshipping God,
> why not get started now? Ya' know—just to get in practice!

Yes, our God is a gathering God, but He's also a scattering God. At Shinar, the Upper Room, and Jerusalem, God told His people to scatter—to spread out and take His name and His glory all over the earth. He wasn't pleased with their man-made flashmobs designed to thwart His worldwide plans of launching His children out across the entire planet to give *every* human being a chance to be part of His ultimate flashmob—the one around the throne in heaven someday. The Lord took some pretty drastic steps to get His people out of the stands and into the game. Take the test below to find out if you're a player—or just a spectator.

A Final Questionnaire:

1. Will you be at the throne? How do you *know* for sure?
2. Do you spend *daily* time worshipping Jesus, the Lamb of God?
3. Have you "scattered", so that God can use *you* to reach the unreached?
4. Are you "co-gathering" with God, recruiting others to join you at the eternal flashmob?

Sorry, you'll have to grade yourself. I gotta' go. I need to log on to the internet and post an upcoming flashmob. This is how it will read:

Let's all meet in heaven,
around the throne of Jesus Christ, the Lamb of God.

Bring a white robe, a palm branch,
and your favorite worship songs.

Oh…and pass the word.
We want this to be the biggest and best flashmob ever!

The Box:
List the people in your life who you feel burdened to pray for, challenge, witness, recruit, etc…to be around the throne *with* you someday.

Three Obstacles to Finding Your North Star: From College to Life!

"MOST STUDENTS COME OUT OF COLLEGE WITH BOTH FEET firmly planted in mid-air!" so says Dr. Howard Hendricks, renowned Dallas Theological Seminary Professor. Your response to the prof might be, "But I thought college was supposed to guide me and point me in the right direction to go in life!" I have seen this combination of fear and feeling lost played out many times for students as they finish high school, college, even graduate programs. School was safe and secure, but now that they're being booted out of the nest, many students have no idea which way to fly.

It's hard to look at the future positively, not pessimistically. Many times I view life as a glass half empty, rather than half full. It's an opportunity of a lifetime to graduate from college and go and accomplish anything and everything you put your mind and heart into. That's the good news. But there's some bad too, and I want to warn you against choosing some of the more toxic options that could end up slowly poisoning your life and future. Here are three common ones:

Obstacle #1: The rocking chair mentality

Many American Christians, out of an extreme view of God's sovereignty and our lack of responsibility, don't embrace the unbelievable partnership the Lord is offering them to know Him and take action. Instead, they choose to spend their college or adult years patiently rocking away, just watching God's "kingdom-building parade" just float by. Maybe it's not their theology that paralyzes them, but their laziness, ignorance or preoccupation with the things of this world. Whatever the reason, let's not waste our life doing nothing and someday face a Creator who will ask us to give an account of *how* we filled our few short years on this earth.

Obstacle #2: Climbing the wrong ladder

These are the ambitious people who aren't satisfied to just ignore or even watch history; no, they want to *make* history. Only problem is, they don't know how! Convinced that hard work, perseverance and getting the right breaks are the key to their success, they'll spend the better part of their life scrambling to get to the top of the ladder, only to look back and realize they were climbing the wrong ladder! My dad had this disheartening experience as he spent thirty years rising in the ranks of an international company, retiring early with a big pension, then going to his obligatory retirement party, complete with cake and watch. That first day on "Easy Street" was when he finally had a moment to look back down the ladder at his life. And the result? He went into depression, realizing that he had nothing of real, lasting value to show for his efforts. Soon afterwards he committed his life to Christ and completely revamped his definition of success. *Now* is the time to figure out what ladder God wants you to get on—and stay on!

Obstacle #3: Dabbling at forty things

Busy Christians in college may once again find their schedule about to explode once they get out into a community and start their careers. Working from the equation that busyness = importance, they not only volunteer for all the extra assignments at work, but also join every civic club, sports team, Bible study, and single's class they can. In their "spare time" they help with the youth group, church greeters, and soup kitchen. Hoping that this whirlwind of activities is somehow going to please God, these "dabblers" are stretched to the point of breaking. Quality time with the Lord and any real, *indepth* ministry fades away.

> The solution is to attempt to focus on a few things
> and do them well. Start now learning how to say "No!"
> on a daily basis, just to keep in practice!

Now that you know what direction you *don't* want to go, we can now have a chat about what direction you *do* want to go! One of the biggest favors you can do for yourself is to work through a personal purpose statement. Once you have biblically and prayerfully put this "life objective" together, use it as a grid to run every decision, job offer, dating prospect, financial situation, etc… through to see if it lines up with God's will for your life.

Finding Your North Star

One night, after a grand performance, a reporter interviewed the featured violinist, asking, "Ms., you *undoubtedly* are the world's greatest concert violinist. *How* did you become the world's greatest concert violinist?"

"Planned neglect!" she quickly answered.

"Planned neglect? *What* do you mean?" he pressed.

"I mean that throughout my entire life, I have planned to neglect *everything* that didn't help me become the world's greatest concert violinist."

You too are going to have to neglect some things, good things, in order to find the time and energy to craft a worthy life objective statement and then, even more importantly, carry through with it. So, take a day and get away to a cabin or park or even a back bedroom away from people, music, TV, and Facebook. Grab your Bible and notepad and spend hours looking up and praying over passages that deal with your walk with God and His assignment for you in this life. Here are three examples of a Biblically based, well-worded life objective statement:

A. The Westminister Shorter Catechism touches on a great theme: "Man's chief end is to glorify God and enjoy Him forever."

B. As I've mentioned, one that I've used for years: "To glorify God through knowing Christ and making Him known."

C. Mark Lewis, a friend with the Navigators campus ministry, came up with: "To glorify God by raising up spiritual generations of leaders flowing from the campus to the U.S. and the nations."

Wow, mine seems a little weak compared to Mark's, but hey, we all have room to grow, right? And once the Lord and you come up with this personal purpose statement, you can then confidently stroll up to the huge conveyer belt of life. After prayerfully examining all the myriad of options whizzing past, you can now make very wise choices, saying, "No." "No." "No." and then finally shouting, "Aha! Yes! This *one* helps me fulfill my life objective!" Without second guessing, you pick it up, put it in your pocket, and into your life. You are on your way to becoming a man or a woman on a very strategic mission from God.

P.S. Maybe you've been to a talk or workshop on "How to Discern the Will of God" where you get tips on unlocking the secret plans God has for your future. I believe the word of God reveals the will of God and my contention is you can cast aside some people's version of Christian fortune telling in favor of following a *biblically* based life objective. It can be your "North Star," helping guide you in the directions and decisions God wants you to be making. Yes, listen to the Lord and be sensitive to His leading, but if He's already clearly given us His marching orders in black and white, why are so many Christians still waiting for an emotional experience to *really* tell us what God wants us to do? The truth is many of us spend time waiting on God when, in fact, He is waiting on us!

Jumping from college to life isn't so tough. God does love you and has a wonderful plan for your life. Turn to Him and His word, and He will show you the way.

"Thy word is a lamp to my feet and a light to my path."
(Psalm 119:105)

The Box:
Write down a key verse or two you might want to use to develop *God's* "north star" for you.

Bonus:
From these verses craft a "north star" life objective statement for you.

NOW, GO FOR IT!

Bonus Features

Other Recommended Books for Students

Live Life on Purpose by Claude Hickman

Blue Like Jazz by Donald Miller

Let the Nations Be Glad by John Piper

Don't Waste Your Life by John Piper

Evangelism Outside the Box by Rick Richardson

How to Successfully Minister to Fraternity and Sorority Men and Women by Isaac Jenkins (For copies email Isaac.Jenkins@uscm.org)

Disciples are Made not Born by Walt Henrichsen

How to Stay Christian in College by J. Budziszewski

Ask Me Anything: Provocative Answers for College Students by J. Budziszewski

Money Matters Workbook for College Students by Larry Burkett and Todd Temple

Knowledge of the Holy by A.W. Tozer

I Kissed Dating Goodbye by Joshua Harris

I Gave Dating a Chance: A Biblical Perspective to Balance the Extremes by Jeramy Clark

Master Plan of Evangelism by Robert Coleman

Reach the U: A Handbook for Effective Campus Ministry by Dennis Gaylor

Following Jesus in the "Real World": Discipleship for the Post-College Years by Richard Lamb

Campus Aflame: A History of Evangelical Awakenings in Collegiate Communities by J. Edwin Orr

A Ready Defense by Josh McDowell

Basic Christianity by John R. W. Scott

Evidence That Demands a Verdict by Josh McDowell

Mere Christianity by C. S. Lewis

More Than a Carpenter by Josh McDowell

Daws by Betty Skinner

Topical Memory System by The Navigators

Unveiled at Last by Bob Sjogren

Cat and Dog Theology by Bob Sjogren and Gerald Robison

Operation World by Patrick Johnstone

Bruchko by Bruce Olson

The Hour that Changes the World by Dick Eastman

From Jerusalem to Irian Jaya by Ruth Tucker

The Creation of a Student Movement by Timothy Wallstrom

The Pursuit of Holiness by Jerry Bridges

The Lost Art of Disciplemaking by Leroy Eims

Developing the Leader Within You by John Maxwell

The 21 Indispensable Qualities of a Leader by John Maxwell

The 21 Irrefutable Laws of Leadership by John Maxwell

I Am Not But I Know I AM: Welcome to the Story of God by Louie Giglio

Wired: For a Life of Worship by Louie Giglio

First Love by Bill Bright

In the Gap by David Bryant

How To Lead Small Groups by Neal F. McBride

Web Links for Students

The Navigators *http://www.navigators.org/*

Reformed University Fellowship *http://www.ruf.org/*

Campus Outreach *http://www.campusoutreach.org/*

Every Nation Campus Ministries *http://www.vcm.com/*

Great Commission Campus Ministries *http://www.gcmweb.org/*

Coalition for Christian Outreach *http://www.ccojubille.org/*

Campus Church Network *http://www.campuschurch.net/*

Campus Renewal Ministries *http://www.campusrenewal.org/*

Student Volunteer Movement 2 *http://www.svm2.net/*

Adventures in Missions *http://www.adventures.org/*

Haystack Prayer Movement *http://www.haystack.org/*

Cafe 10/40 *http://www.cafe1040.com/*

Teach Overseas *http://www.teachoverseas.org/*

iWitness *http://www.igoglobal.org/*

United World Mission (Expedition237) *http://www.expedition237.org/*

Baptist Student Ministries *http://www.student.org/*

Chi Alpha *http://www.chialpha.com/*

Christ for the Nations *http://www.cfni.org/*

Heart of God Ministries *http://www.heartofgod.com/flash/*

Right Now Campaign *http://www.rightnow.org/*

NVision Mission Seminars *http://www.thebodybuilders.net/nvision*

Brigada *http://www.brigada.org/*

A.D. 2000 *http://www.ad2000.org/*

Global Mapping *http://www.gmi.org/*

U.S. Center for World Mission *http://www.uscwm.org/*

Mission Frontiers Magazine *http://www.missionfrontiers.org/*

Global Prayer Digest *http://www.global-prayer-digest.org/*

World Christian Database *http://worldchristiandatabase.org/wcd/*

Joshua Project *http://www.joshuaproject.net/*

Perspectives *http://www.perspectives.org/*

Passion Network *http://www.268generation.com/*

Ethnologue *http://www.ethnologue.com/*

Revival Resource Center *http://www.watchword.org/*

American Bible Society *http://www.bibles.com/*

Boundless Webzine *http://www.boundless.org/*

Campus Crusade for Christ *http://www.uscm.org/*

Evangelism Tool Box *http://www.evangelismtoolbox.com/*

Everystudent.com *http://www.everystudent.com/*

4 Greeks.org *http://www.4greeks.org/*

Intervarsity Christian Fellowship *http://www.ivcf.org/*

Leadership University *http://www.leaderu.com/*

The Traveling Team *http://www.thetravelingteam.org/*

Passion Network *http://www.268generation.com/*

Reach the U *http://www.reachtheu.com/*

Short Term Missions.com *http://www.shorttermmissions.com/*

Student Mobilization *http://www.stumo.org/*

Veritas Forum *http://www.veritas.org/index.htm/*

World Religions Index *http://wri.leaderu.com*

Campus Christianity *http://www.campuschristianity.com/*

Watchword *http://www.watchword.org/*

Voice of the Martyrs *http://www.persecution.com/*

Discover the Book *http://www.discoverthebook.org/*

God Squad *http://www.godsquad.com/*

Waymore *http://www.waymore.org/*

Methodist Campus Ministries *http://www.gbhem.org/asp/campusMin.asp/*

Lutheran Campus Ministries *http://www.wels.net/cgi-bin/site.
pl?campusMinistry/*

His House Christian Fellowships *http://www.hhcf.org/*

Fellowship of Christian Athletes *http://www.fca.org/*

Youth With a Mission *http://www.ywam.org/*

Nazarene Campus Ministries *http://www.nazscm.org/*

Evangelical Free Campus Ministries *http://www.efca.org/student/*

Relevant Magazine *http://www.relevantmagazine.com/*

Christian Post Webzine *http://www.christianpost.com/*

Young Life *http://www.younglife.org/*

Youth for Christ *http://www.yfc.org/*

Athletes in Action *http://www.aia.com/*

How to Order More Copies of This Book

Go to **BrownLikeCoffee.com** and order as many as you like. You get two choices:

 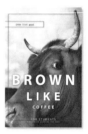

To place your order e mail us at **Jack@BrownLikeCoffee.com**

You don't know Jack? That's o.k. That's not her/his real name anyway.

Have your credit card ready.

Remember every penny of profit from the sale of this book goes into mission efforts to expand the Kingdom of God around the world. Thanks!

Prices:

1 copy: $10.99

2-10 copies: $9.99

11-30 copies: $8.99

31 or more: $7.99

(S&H will be determined by your location.)